Supporting Children's Creativity Through Music, Dance, Drama and Art

Creative conversations in the early years

Edited by
Fleur Griffiths

LONDON AND NEW YORK

First published 2010
by Routledge
2 Park Square, Milton Park, Abingdon, Oxon OX14 4RN

Simultaneously published in the USA and Canada
by Routledge
270 Madison Avenue, New York, NY 10016

Routledge is an imprint of the Taylor & Francis Group, an informa business

Typeset in Bembo by Taylor & Francis Books
Printed and bound in Great Britain by
The MPG Books Group Ltd

British Library Cataloguing in Publication Data
A catalogue record for this book is available from the British Library

Library of Congress Cataloging in Publication Data
Supporting children's creativity through music, dance, drama and art : creative conversations in the early years / edited by Fleur Griffiths.
p. cm.
Includes index.
1. Arts – Study and teaching (Early childhood) 2. Creative ability in children. I. Griffiths, Fleur.
LB1139.5.A78S87 2010
372.5'044 – dc22
2009019495

ISBN 10: 0-415-48963-2 (hbk)
ISBN 10: 0-415-48966-0 (pbk)

ISBN 13: 978-0-415-48965-2 (hbk)
ISBN 13: 978-0-415-48966-9 (pbk)

I am certain of nothing but the holiness of the heart's affections and the truth of the imagination

(Keats, letter to Benjamin Bailey, 2 November 1817)

The sense of wonder that we are all born with – a sensitivity to the look and feel and sound of things – matters a great deal. If we try to look at things with children, if we value the moments when they stop and stare and wonder at the world, then we probably do more for their creative, aesthetic and artistic development than a host of specific art exercises might ever do.

(Kolbe 2007: 11)

Contents

Acknowledgements

This book has emerged thanks to my collaborators and colleagues, children and staff in early years settings in the north-east of England, especially:

- Bensham Bank Community Nursery School (Gateshead)
- Dunston Hill Community Primary School (Gateshead)
- Houghton Community Nursery School (Sunderland)
- Hylton Redhouse Nursery School (Sunderland)
- Lingey House Primary School (Gateshead)
- Roman Road Primary School (Gateshead)
- Rossmere Primary (Hartlepool)
- Saint Aidan's Church of England Primary School (Hartlepool)
- Tweedmouth Primary West First School (Berwick, Northumberland),

with the backing of Linda Tallent, Sue Johnson and Kay Rooks;

- to the three Annes from Northumberland LA: Anne Robins, Anne Robertson and Anne Rutherford;
- to a host of schools in the borough of Westminster;
- to the inspiration of a visit to Italy to Reggio Emilia's preschools;
- to the heart-warming experience of Annabella's Wonderland in Cluj, Romania.
- Closer to home, I could not have done without the support of my mentoring friend, Pat Triggs; my empathetic daughter Esther Griffiths and my patient partner John Lowe.
- I needed Oliver to rocket me to the moon and stars from his living-room sofa!

Collaborators

Stephanie Brandon worked in the education system for almost 30 years as a teacher of all subjects and ages, with experience of nursery, community and liaison work, as well as many years as music coordinator in a large primary school. As a primary school head-teacher, she was obliged to raise standards while being deeply committed to the development of the whole child in a joyful and creative learning environment. She currently works for The Sage Gateshead, a new bastion of radical and innovative thinking in terms of musical creativity, to develop an exciting programme of participatory work in music for under-5s. As Head of Early Years and Family Learning, she now supports many aspects of The Sage Gateshead's Learning and Participation Programme through example, training and delivery across the UK's North-East region.

Annabella Cant is an educational trainer, founder of a charity in Romania, and director of her own humanitarian pre-school since 1999. She has completed studies at Babes-Bolyai University, Cluj-Napoca (Faculty of Psychology and Science of Education and Faculty of Letters) and a Master's degree at Simon Fraser University of Vancouver, Canada, under the supervision of Prof. Dr Kieran Egan (Faculty of Education). During 15 years of practice she has developed her own teaching technique, derived from the new educational philosophy, Imaginative Education. As a trainer, she presents workshops for teachers and parents about new and better ways of teaching and raising young children. She has published three children's books, a trilingual educational dictionary, and articles in educational journals in Romania.

Rose Davies began teaching in a nursery class in County Durham in 1978. She then taught in schools serving diverse communities in London and Derby. Following a few years of parenting her young, she worked as the Family Literacy coordinator in Derby and then taught reception-aged children for several years. In 2003 she returned to the North-East, to the post of Area Special Educational needs Co-ordinator with Gateshead Local Authority. She now teaches at Bensham Grove Community Nursery School in Gateshead. She says that returning to teach nursery children in the North-East is as though she has rounded the circle in her career, and she finds she is more fascinated than ever by children's learning and development.

Marion Farmer has had a varied career in education. She has worked as a music teacher, a teacher of infants, an educational psychologist specialising in work with children and young people with language and communication disorders, and a university teacher delivering child development, developmental psychology and qualitative research methods courses to undergraduates and postgraduates. She has contributed to and co-authored a number of books and has also published her research in academic journals. Her principal research interest lies in the area of language development and she is particularly interested in children's creativity in the use of language in narrative and play.

Angela Foley is an educational psychologist attached to Gateshead Children's Centres (Sure Start), where she has set up a network of Music and Movement groups for children and their families, and trained staff to work with music. The groups have varied, but parental involvement is vital in all cases. Her interest in children and music developed mainly when she was at home with her children and running a local toddlers' group, and then a music and movement group for parents and children. Then, for four years, she ran a weekly pre-school multi-disciplinary music and movement group for children with additional needs and their parents, and also worked for a short time at an I CAN nursery. Her focus has recently moved to working in nursery and reception class settings where she uses music and music-related activities to help develop children's language, listening, attention and social skills.

Fleur Griffiths is a retired nursery teacher/educational psychologist/senior lecturer in Early Childhood Studies (Sunderland University). In retirement, she has worked as an educational consultant in Foundation Stage settings in Hartlepool and Gateshead local authorities. She devised The Talking Table as a creative context for conversation. Her chief interest has always been language development. Her Bachelor's degree was in English literature (London University, 1961–64) and her first teaching post involved her in team-teaching of topics, using story, art, dance and drama. She focused on children with special needs and trained as an educational psychologist at Queen's University of Belfast in1979. In the north-east of England (1979–2003), she had specialist roles in language units, and at the I CAN nursery, working with parents. Parents have always been a priority for her, and she welcomed the responsibility of Parent Partnership Officer in North Tyneside. She has contributed to training for teachers in Hartlepool on the courses: Listening to Children (Lancaster and Broadbent, 2003) and Communicating Matters (DfES). This last owes much to the collaborative book *Communication Counts; speech and language in the early years* (2002), which is a key text.

Kate Louise Harbottle qualified as a teacher with the Gateshead Initial Teacher Training and currently works as a reception class teacher in the Early Years Team at Dunston Hill Community Primary School in Gateshead. Previous to this, she completed a BTEC Diploma in Early Childhood Studies and worked as a nursery nurse with Newcastle City Council, before completing a BA Honours degree in Care and Education of Very Young Children at the University of Northumbria.

Karen Hayon is a speech and language therapist who has been working in early years settings in Westminster, London for the past eleven years. As well as her role within her local NHS department, she is currently working as an Early Language Consultant on the government initiative *Every Child a Talker.*

Chris Holmes is an early years educator and professional photographer with ten years' experience in the field of arts and education. Her role at Sightlines Initiative, the UK reference point for Reggio Children, involves developing and managing early years creativity projects, as well as producing exhibits and project narratives for the continuing professional development field. Chris also works in a freelance capacity in the field of documentary and commercial photography.

Marysia Holubecki-France is currently a team leader of the Mental Health In Education research and development team in County Durham. The team delivers a range of parent-and-child programmes, some of which incorporate significant work/coaching/training with teachers. She works closely with colleagues in CAMHS (Children and Adult Mental Health Services), aiming to improve relationships, resilience and well-being. She has completed the CBT (Cognitive Behaviour Therapy) training required to carry out such programmes as The Mellow Parenting Programme and The Webster Stratton Incredible Years Programme. Previously she headed a Behaviour Support Team as an advisory teacher. She approaches her interest in communication difficulties from a BA degree in philosophy, which she followed up with an MA (Sheffield University) on communication style in 2002.

Tracy Kirkbride qualified as a teacher at Ripon and York St John and specialised in English literature. She is currently an assistant head teacher of a large primary school in Hartlepool, with specific responsibility for the early years. Prior to this, Tracy worked in a variety of areas and has experience as a Foundation Stage leader in a primary school and as a nursery teacher in a preparatory school nursery. During her time as an early years teacher, Tracy has developed a keen interest in the learning environment. Study trips to Reggio Emilia and research projects towards a Masters in Education have instilled in her the goal constantly to pursue the best for the children within her care in a rapidly changing world.

Alison Martin gained a BA (Hons) degree at Leeds University in 1991. She worked with adults with mental health issues, moving on to work with young people experiencing emotional and behavioural difficulties, and their families. In 2001 she qualified as a teacher from Edinburgh University. She now works in Hartlepool as a Foundation Stage teacher and runs weekly workshops for parents.

Ken Patterson studied Psychology and Biological Sciences (BSc) at Edinburgh (1975–1978). He won the Newcastle University PGCE prize for his dissertation exploring the use of puppetry in primary education in 1983. After work as a primary class teacher and music coordinator, he became Advisory Teacher for Primary Music in Newcastle upon Tyne local authority in 1990. This provided opportunities to lead the Quayside Arts Project and Arts Focus, working with artists-in-residence and teachers working in partnership. In 1996 he became Arts Coordinator at Wingrove Primary School in the west end of Newcastle. Self-employed since 1999, he coordinated Making Music On the Line, a millennium project with Channel 4, Oxfam, Folkworks and others. That same year, he worked with jazz musicians at the Big People Festival Educational Programme, developing *Jazz Building Blocks* (2005). He was a key member of the Comusica team of lead community musicians at The Sage Gateshead in 2001, the North East's international venue and music centre. In 2007 he co-directed 4 Corners Music, working with Northumberland Music Service and Creative Partnerships in a project call Jazz Attack which sought evidence of children's improvisation in fourteen schools across the county. He acts and writes the music in a number of Theatre sans Frontières productions and collaborates with storyteller Chris Bostock in *Tales for the Turning Year*, a cycle of the seasons in story and music.

Kay Rooks's work in early years education spans 27 years. Having trained as a teacher in 1983, she specialised in language development, receiving the Diploma in Child Language and Disability from Newcastle University in 2004 As an advisory teacher, she currently works in Sunderland, engaged in professional training of teachers using various programmes: Talk Talk; Listening to Children; Communicating Matters and the most recent, *Every Child a Talker*. Her projects include Educational Action Zone (EAZ) initiatives and creative projects with Sightlines (Reggio Children in UK).

Evi Typadi qualified as a speech and language therapist from University College London in 1997. She has been working in early years settings in Westminster, London for the past eight years. She is currently working as an Early Language Consultant on the government initiative *Every Child a Talker*. Her particular interests are adult–child interaction in early years' settings and learning English as an additional language.

Introduction

Fleur Griffiths

> Value should be placed on contexts, communicative processes, and the construction of a wide network of reciprocal exchanges among children and between children and adults.
>
> (Malaguzzi in conversation in Edwards et al. 1998: 68)

'Concentrating on conversation between adults and children is an absolute priority'

This headline in the *Guardian* caught my attention. It sprung from the page because it chimed in with my long-term commitment to such conversations, to those reciprocal exchanges. The article highlighted the growing awareness in early years education of the need for adults and children to engage in creative conversations across the art forms, to use the many languages of children: their gestures and body movements, their drawings and musical rhythms, as well as their words. Children need listening adults who will take turns to create shared meanings in playful contexts. Practitioner guidance is strongly needed at this time on creative ways to implement the themes of the new Foundation Stage Framework, i.e. listening together; playing and learning outdoors; music and dance; number, shapes and problem solving; being me; and mark making and representation.

Early years practitioners have a tradition of valuing play as the vehicle for learning, but tensions have developed between 'getting on' in terms of measurable individual attainments and 'getting on with others' through social learning and joint meaning making. Pressures to attain set targets and reach certain objectives have concerned parents and teachers, sometimes to the detriment of the enjoyment of learning. The agenda has become increasingly set by adults to inform rather than to discover the interests and pre-occupations of children. Anxieties about attainment as individuals have been transmitted to parents, who would usually be more attuned to the happiness of their children, how they interact with others and whether they belong. Better to involve adults as partners and co-constructors of meaning. More can be done with *respect* for children's abilities and predispositions as the base, and the making of a *reciprocal* and *resourceful* learning context as the means. These three Rs – Respect, Reciprocity and Resourcefulness – characterise the relationship in which the traditional three Rs can flourish.

This book aims to put the joy and excitement back into the learning process and to celebrate the creative capacities of young children, given proper support and opportunities. To do this, I depend on my creative friends and colleagues. We are reflective practitioners, who have based our work on the premise that children are naturally curious and prone to be social. We value the reciprocal encounters we have with children, and we have detailed these 'creative conversations'.

As in the previous collaborative book, *Communication Counts* (Griffiths 2002), we have met socially for 'Dinner Dialogues' at my house to generate ideas and reflect on our practice of creativity, and have come to new understandings in the heat of the exchange. Conversation, at its best, is about such meetings of minds and the challenge of facing new perspectives. Our conversations touch on major questions expressed as queries:

- How do you recognise creativity in children?
- How do you foster it?
- When do you stand back, and when intervene?
- What are the structures that allow the safety to be creative?
- What are legitimate risks?
- How do we ensure there is time and space available?
- How do we extend and exploit possibilities?
- How do we balance the needs and skills of individuals and the group?
- How does creativity fit in with the Guidelines and with other statutory demands?
- Is creativity a matter of special talent and the province of a few? Can everyone be imaginative?
- How does a creative impulse become skilled? How are such skills taught?
- What to do with the products? How to celebrate them? Document them?

The process of writing this book reflects the creative process we engage in with children. We were unable to say in advance exactly what the content of the chapters would be, but we trusted that it would *evolve* as we exchanged views at our Dinner Dialogues and we took the risk. We do not claim to have simple answers, so anyone looking for easy solutions will be disappointed; but anyone keen to engage in similar *conversations* will find the thinking journey absorbing – and children truly wonderful and amazing in their inventiveness.

The collaborators

My collaborators have shared their learning journeys in education and that is why our writing has taken a biographical rather than an academic route. I introduce them where possible, using their words from our conversations. I try to bring them to life, from the list of contributors at the beginning, and use their first names.

Two life experiences this year have inspired my thinking about creative conversations: a visit to Annabella's Wonderland Nursery in Cluj, Romania, and to Reggio Emilia in Italy, renowned for its creative pedagogy. Friends made on these trips contribute directly to the book. **Annabella** considers what the words on her nursery fence – 'welcome', 'magic', 'wonder' – mean in practice. She shows how important it is for teachers to enter the imaginative world of children. The power of the imagination can often override limited resources. In fact, too many toys and too much choice can constrict the imagination. We have all had the experience of a young child preferring the box and wrappings to the gift. Their play sends a message to us about their priorities.

We are keen to pick up on such messages. We observe children with an open mind, making efforts to understand and to discover the child's meanings. We listen to their voices and actions. We try to make learning visible through photos, tape recordings, stories and observations, and we are especially lucky to have **Chris**'s telling photographs.

Rose contributes such observations from her nursery. She can sense when the children are engaged in meaningful creation, whether painting, singing, dancing or constructing; whether alone or enacting scenarios with friends. She shared 'Dancing on the Decking', at our first gathering, describing the purposeful turn taking of two boys as 'a conversation going on, as they wove in and out of each other'. This account and examples of her daily observations can be found in the book. She adopted the overhead projector (set up in my living room at one Dinner Dialogue meeting) for use with her children to create artistic patterns from recycled materials, aesthetically presented, as practised in Reggio Emilia. This created a 'dialogue with intelligent materials' as the children selected, arranged and improvised: they could add and subtract and exchange; they could explore and develop; they could scrap an idea without any sense of making a mistake. They could join things together inventively with ribbon or paperclips. They were not confined by convention or adult expectation and could get pleasing effects by lucky juxtapositions. In the words of a five-year-old child at Reggio Emilia:

> To transform something, you need brilliant ideas.

Kay's notion of what creativity means has been enlarged over the years and been transformed by her experience of Reggio and the role it gives to the artist in the 'atelier' (studio) within the school building. She describes projects bringing visiting artists and musicians to work creatively with children in school. However, the first step on her learning journey was to talk less and listen more, so as to discover the meanings of children. She marvels at the way children make sense of what goes on in a conversation:

> My earliest recollection of listening to the children more and talking less was a conversation between myself and two girls, Natalie and Janine, both aged three years, as we sat at the drawing table. Natalie described her family summer holiday to Turkey and talked in great depth about their yacht named the *Monte Rosa*. She talked fondly about 'Nanny', whom I wrongly guessed to be her grandma, and the activities she, Nanny and her brother experienced. I consciously tried not to lead the conversation but to make comments and appropriate gestures to indicate listening. Janine sat quietly throughout this conversation and then made one comment: 'When I was sick there was turkey in it'. It was a wonderful demonstration of the connections that children make between words, in this case 'turkey', and their marvellous ability to apply logic. It also helped me appreciate the varied experience of life children possess at three years of age, and that we cannot assume shared knowledge of life.

Tracy has managed to do that difficult thing of planting ideas – familiar to those who extol the virtues of Reggio Emilia's creative pedagogy – into a different cultural soil and keeping alive a vibrant learning context. She communicates her philosophy of teaching and learning in a tape-recorded conversation. As with all transcripts, the version cannot do full justice to the meeting of minds on this occasion, because it cannot convey the shared glances, the laughter, the emphatic bang of the fist on the table, the pregnant pauses, the excited dash of words. It confines communication to words on a page, when we know that there are many languages operating in any conversation. It is a testimony to the clarity of her educational vision that her message comes across in spite of these restrictions. In her class of five-year-olds, she builds a climate of *trust* in which children take responsibility, with the adults, for their environment. As she says:

> They trust in me that their things will be there tomorrow. So if they need to finish off a picture, or add to it or work into it, their picture will be there tomorrow. It won't be in the bin! They will know where to find it because they trust in the environment. That environment supports their learning – it is not settled by the adult. Leave it in a safe place and it is there because it is their environment as well as ours. And I think that as much as we do to make an environment look lovely and aesthetically pleasing to others, we are actually ruining the learning opportunities of our children, because that's not what they want.

Marysia alerts us to the delights and dangers of adult involvement in children's drawing and how easily even well-meaning adults can misguidedly intervene. She set us thinking about the role of the adult by showing us her son Oliver's pictures and paintings. He loves to tell and act the story of his marks and lines and careful dashes of colour. They are dramatic and dynamic constructions of battles in space or exciting journeys and they are capable of being extended with sensitive adult feedback and interest. A girl of the same age draws a beautifully executed picture of a neat row of flowers on a band of green grass beneath a band of blue sky. Every adult can see what it represents, so comments have probably been restricted to praise for neatness, thereby perpetuating the same production. Does this mean that she cannot develop her imagination and is trapped within a sterile skill? Schooling leads Oliver to play the accepted game, and to colour in the lines of a picture given him with little relevance to his interests. When asked by his teacher to draw a picture about their visit to the cheese market, he filled most of the space with dabs of blue rain, the drenching being the most important feature of the trip; market stall and sellers were squashed in dutifully when he realised he was on the wrong track! In conversation, Marysia conveyed her deep concern about missed opportunities:

> We talk about a broad, balanced curriculum, but what about a rich curriculum, that's the thing that's missing. If you explore *every* opportunity that a child gives you, whether it's music, a picture, a line, a mark or whatever, if you take it to its natural conclusion, which could be in a variety of ways, you will find a huge amount, if you are interested and enthusiastic at the right time. And give feedback like all good behaviour modification programmes; if you're giving them some positive feedback, they will carry on doing more rather than less of it. It worries me that some children, without that kind of encouragement live within much narrower boundaries.

My contribution is 'Creative conversations: the Talking Table', which allows children to speak, draw, enact or sing a song in the service of joint story telling. I work on the premise that focusing solely on spoken language impedes communication, especially for shy and withdrawn children. I believe that the 'Watch/Do' turn-taking pattern of mothers and toddlers needs to be established before the 'Listen/Speak' exchange that marks verbal conversation. It involves the many languages of children: their gestures and body language; their drawing and drama to create shared meanings round the Table and to give voice to unspoken communication and emotion. The circle-time routines give shape to the encounter and allow each child the chance to show, tell, enact or simply participate by passing an interesting object around the group. The role of the adult is to listen, and to facilitate turn taking and to ensure that each child feels welcome and befriended. An A–Z of children from Adam to Zoë, story vignettes of the children who have visited the Table during the five years it has been operating in nurseries in the North-East of England, can be found throughout the book. These stories illustrate the range of children involved and the flexibility of the adult in including all comers. I have found the circle-time structure helpful to me because it puts the authority into the pattern and saves me from being a controller. In dialogue, I remembered:

> When I was being trained, there was an emphasis on free expression so there would be loads of exciting materials for children to use, but this did not guarantee creativity. Unless children know how glue works, or scissors work, there can be complete chaos. It may be very novel and creative to take a paint brush and tickle the hamster with it, but the paintbrush has a purpose, a skilled purpose. So, it is always trying to get a balance between allowing that freedom of expression, that unique use of materials and arrangements and having some kind of shape into which you can put these ideas. Being the sort of person I am – not being very authoritative – I have to put quite a lot of authority into the 'shape', like turns. Otherwise they would all press on me, sit on my lap, and want my full attention and they would never become a creative group, proud of their authoring of group stories. So, there is a tension all the time.

Others have adopted the Talking Table and **Ali** and **Kate** contribute their adaptations and transcripts of children talking. As Ali says, 'the turn-taking pattern round the circle gives the safety in which children can be creative.' She unrolls before us the communal paper of drawings, marks, and her written recordings and demonstrates, 'there are stories in all of these marks the children have made'. Children's understandings cut across all the artificial boundaries which our disciplines dictate. Their many languages intertwine to make sense for them. Kate reports, 'We have found the notion of the Talking Table to be a fantastic way to encourage focused speaking and listening, mark making, turn taking and storytelling skills – a quality time for all.'

Evi and **Karen** have adopted the Talking Table because it fits with their understanding that meaning is constructed socially. They chart their professional journey as speech and language therapists away from medical models, to a focus on social interaction in language learning. They owe much to Vivian Paley, the kindergarten teacher who brought her classrooms to life by honouring the words and ideas of children. Her book *The Boy who*

Would be a Helicopter provides the launch-pad for the *helicopter* technique. This is the starting point for their narrative and dramatic work with groups of young children. They have created a tool for developing children's confidence, curiosity, creativity and communication skills which is usable by teachers.

Angela writes of her own learning journey in creating music and movement groups for young children in children's centres. She saw what worked with her own children at home, and transferred her insights to her professional arena as an educational psychologist. Because she is a visitor in these settings she, of necessity, has to carry out structured sessions – when she would prefer to intersperse music more flexibly into the unfolding of the day's events. She conveys the value of seeing the whole child, and the prime importance of promoting well-being and social confidence if creativity is to flourish. She asserts the power of communicating through music. She picks up on body movements and gestures that start non-verbal interactions, with children responding and inventing in the encounter. This ability is not based on being a talented musician, but on the communication skills that lie within the repertoire of anyone who loves to work with children. She is strong in disclaiming her own musical skill, and believes that the confidence of many practitioners has been dented by elitist attitudes in music education. Her aim in her writing is to bring ease and enjoyment into the grasp of any early years worker. In conversation, she explained:

> I've been very lucky; the more I do, the more creative it can become. By being creative, you give other people permission to start questioning what they do. I say to them, 'If you do just one more thing differently this term, things will change gradually.'

She passes on the strategies and ideas that have inspired her, and discusses with **Stephanie** (whose workshops she has attended) the kind of structure that allows children the opportunity to create musically. Steph is horrified when musical instruments are left in the music corner, a free-for-all, and often mistreated; quickly she saw the benefits of a careful introduction and experimentation with instruments, with children drawn together round a cloth, 'conversing' with the adult. As she says,

> It has never failed to delight me to see how even the very youngest children respond to safe, fair, supportive structures like the circle ... When children make the structure their own (and they do), they are learning how to use their growing knowledge and experience in ways which feed them and their creativity. They can make proper, informed choices about their creative opportunities rather than swimming in a swamp of whim and caprice.

Ken brought his drum to dinner and he had a drum conversation with Peter, a visitor from Kenya, on his African drum. They listened to each other and improvised and elaborated, as do jazz musicians. He shows how the same can be done with children using his jazz 'building blocks'. He has worked in many cultures and brings the participatory style of much world music, like 'call and response', into use with young children. Once children are comfortable with these easy echoes, they then can improvise and invent. He wants teachers to be equally confident:

> What is important is having the confidence to set up structures and then to stand back and set children free to create. I often talk about the 'devising classroom' where such open-endedness is the name of the game. It is hard for teachers to give over the lead to children and to be there just to facilitate, not to direct.

He also refers to these strategies as forming a 'palette' of possibility for future improvisation. This repertoire can be reworked as children grow older and more skilled, in a learning 'spiral'.

It is significant that Ken uses metaphors from other art forms to explain musical practices. We need to explain ourselves in new ways using new metaphors: the teaching/learning process needs to be seen as 'scaffolding' or 'weaving' rather than 'funnelling', 'packaging' or 'transmitting' of ideas.

Marion reviews the developmental psychological research that has bearing on conversation making. She asks: 'What do creative conversations require of children? What do they require of adults? What are the consequences for children and adults? What is created?' She finishes her piece by noting the current press for a return to creative approaches, which indicates that creativity is valued for both its social and its economic benefits.

For the Reflections in Chapter 9, I quote **Rose** talking about what she has learned about creativity by being part of the Dinner Dialogues. She no longer feels limited by guidelines from government:

> The six areas of learning and development need not limit us in terms of our expectations of what children will do with particular resources or activities. They can help us to see children's development more holistically if we are open to the processes taking place and really tune in to what is happening.

We are not in the position of Reggio educators who can work without external curricula. But we too can be more 'holistic' and 'tune in' to children's thinking to guide our implementation of the curriculum. Like Malaguzzi, we too know that to be with children is to work 'with one-third certainty and two-thirds uncertainty and the new'. We too can be sure, however, that the children are ready to help us by 'offering us ideas, suggestions, problems, questions, clues and paths to follow' especially 'if they trust us and see us as a resource' (Malaguzzi 1998).

Reading and resources

Edwards, C., Gandini, L. and Forman, G. (eds) (1998) *The Hundred Languages of Children: the Reggio Emilia Approach – Advanced Reflections*, London: JAI Press Ltd.

Griffiths, F. (2002) *Communication Counts: Speech and Language Difficulties in the Early Years*, London: David Fulton.

Malaguzzi (1998) cited in *Refocus Journal*, 8 (Spring 2009), 18, www.sightlines-initiative.com.

Welcome, wonder and magic

Words on the fence of a Romanian kindergarten

Annabella Cant

Three colourful wooden characters appear on the fence of our kindergarten in Cluj (Romania): a bear, a strawberry and an apple. On each of these images is painted a word: 'Welcome' on the apple, 'Magic' on the bear and 'Wonder' on the strawberry.

I am connected with these symbols because they define my work, my dreams and my existence. Professionally, they defined my way of teaching, my way of seeing the development of young children. Wonder is present because we are trying to transform concrete and cold meanings into warm and attractive symbols. We try to make children feel welcome to learning in their own way. Children have multiple hidden powers when they enter pre-school. The role of teachers is to make them aware of these powers and show them how to use them. If teachers succeed in doing so, children will keep on discovering the endless world around them in a very easy way. Educational, biological and psychological studies show us that children are much more powerful than adults. Just try to imagine the amount of information they are able to acquire even as helpless babies!

Science has demonstrated that our brain develops to its final size in the first years of life. The speed of development in small children can be compared with a snowball rolling down a mountain. The mountain is very steep, and the snow ball continues to roll down-growing–until it meets a bump. The bump propels it into the air and this is the moment when we, as adults, have to jump in. We have to catch the snow ball and not let it smash to the ground. If we are late or lazy … the snow ball will be damaged for good.

Metaphorically, I show how important our role as parents and teachers actually is in the first years of a child's life. Catching the snow ball in time is actually our way of educating children. During this imperative process we shall not forget to use the necessary constituents of our teaching: welcome, wonder and magic.

Welcome

The first step of an educator in teaching children is not planning, it is not setting the content, and it is not preparing the evaluation. The first step should always be the process of making children feel welcome! If this step is forgotten, all the preparation, planning and curriculum developments will be of no avail. I call this step 'Opening the door'. If we do not open the door, we will experience teaching as banging into a wall over and over again. Opening the door is not a difficult step. I love opening and re-opening the door.

Children love the individual attention of the teacher and of their peers. A heart full of warmth and a face full of real smiles make children feel welcome.

Forget for the moment all external stresses and think only of the children. Do things that involve games, fun, jokes. Make yourself known to the children, connect with them. Making children feel welcomed to education creates the kind of motivation that replaces half of the effort of teaching.

It happens sometimes that the door is locked, and opening it seems impossible. Children with closed doors have experienced difficult moments emotionally. Their trust in anyone has been shattered by somebody or something. I do not panic when this happens. I have been working for the last ten years with emotionally challenged children, and I know that they cannot wait to give you the key to their painfully closed door. They do not like to be locked in, but they need to be introvert in order to cope with the harsh realities around them. So my opinion is to not try to shake their door. Do not try to 'wake them up' and show them the beauty of socialising. It will only strengthen their iron lock. These children are the ones who like to sit alone, play alone, stay close to the door of the classroom. I had a little orphan boy in my class who sat beside the open door of the classroom for two whole school years. He cried every time somebody closed the door. I understood him and accepted his needs because I found their source: the constantly locked and dark doors of the orphanage, the social claustrophobia provoked by the compulsory groups of the orphanage. He was not allowed ever to be alone; he had to be with his peers, talk to them, act socially and hide all his real feelings. For him, coming to our school was an escape! He understood that we would welcome him whatever his state of mind … and he gained courage; the courage to request his needs, the courage to state that he loves to be alone, and that he does not want to see locked doors any more. He needed to see the opening, the freedom that he felt in our school. He needed to know that he could fly if he wanted to, and this is why the door of our classroom was not closed, for two years. Of course he learned to compromise and to negotiate. From a wide-open door he progressed to a one-centimetre-wide open door. I decided to allow him this favour because, first of all, he needed the emotional security for learning, and because all the other children understood his needs and accepted his right to special treatment. It is astonishing to see how the other children have the power and capabilities to understand a fellow child's needs. They seem to have a deep connection to each other that shows them how far something can go.

As well as this little boy in my class, all children have the need to feel welcome and respected. Building the connection with the children is immensely important for the teaching–learning process. Once created, the bridge of trust and comfortableness can take you and the children anywhere in the curriculum.

Having the word 'welcome' on a fence may seem quite a paradox. How can the two concepts coexist? I think it is very interesting to discuss this paradox, because the implications in teaching and learning are important.

What is a fence doing? It is:

- closing in
- limiting
- hiding
- depriving

- discriminating
- constraining
- coercing
- restraining
- keeping out of sight
- forgetting
- imprisoning
- controlling.

All these words could describe our curriculum and the traditional way of teaching. Even if, because of the years of experience, we stop noticing all these features, the effects will be there. All we have to do is to add to it the word 'WELCOME'. This word 'welcome' magically transforms the fence into a 'protective', safe and cosy boundary.

Any curriculum content can be transformed by the magical power that a teacher possesses. Teachers are the lucky ones, who can confer a special mental image to content we teach and are able to provoke emotional responses from the children. Our best tool is the 'story'. Kieran Egan says that 'a story tells you how to feel.' He illustrates this by using this story:

> A girl crossed the street.
> The girl crossed the street to help the little boy who had fallen off his bike.
> She only wanted to help him because she saw that he had a fifty dollar bill poking out of his pocket and wanted to take it.
> The girl had witnessed the boy steal the money from an old lady and was getting the money to return it to the old lady.
> The boy had only stolen the money because his family was very poor and he wanted to help pay for his little sister's hospital bill.
>
> (Egan 2008)

Our feelings about a character change as we read each sentence of a story. We can switch on the narrative mind of children by using emotionally engaging stories in our teaching. The emotions we feel are the affective instruments our memories cling to; they help us to learn and remember. Our creativity allows us to associate meanings to feelings, words to images, concepts to emotions. And the children feel welcome in this world.

It is time to talk about:

Wonder

Wonder is the key to knowledge.
Wonder is willing to know more.
Wonder is questioning everything.
Wonder is the way from the unknown to the possible …

Adding wonder to our curriculum will make … wonders! I have done it endless times and I tell you that it works. Even children at a pre-linguistic level can understand content that has been formed into a narrative. The narrative line can connect subject matters into integrated curriculum content, or it can link components of a lesson in a logical, warm and affective way. The stories I create during a certain theme always start in the class, together with the children. I start guessing their state of mind, their momentary and durable needs, dreams and wishes. All these elements I detect through imaginative games: questions that call forth ideas, images and actions. These creative conversations help children to open up and to share with the class all their feelings or needs.

What is very important during this stage of planning is the teacher's approach. The teacher must adjust vocabulary, intonation and body language to all new situations. Children must feel curiosity and wonder at every moment of the narrative. During the imaginative game, I collect valuable information regarding the needs of the class and, without even stopping the game, I start the 'set theme'. I know that most teachers try to gather information from the internet, from books or existing stories in order to plan their lessons. I would never state that this is wrong, but I would give this advice: start with the children. They provide the most powerful and useful information regarding the direction in which your lesson has to go; and then, use the internet. Here are some examples of how to provoke an imaginative game and how to help children express themselves.

I wonder

- what you dreamt last night;
- what made you smile yesterday;
- whether somebody was crying;
- whether you met animals on the way to school;
- how you make your friends laugh.
- Close your eyes and tell me what do you see (whisper in my ears).
- What would a horse see now in the field?
- What would you like to do if I gave you a blank piece of paper? Why?
- Close your eyes and tell me what feels cold (warm, windy, colourful, heavy, etc.).
- Let's all close our eyes and I'll tell you what I see: I see something blue and very light, what could it be?

All these wonderings 'open the door' of children and let you into their magical world. Once inside, it is time to play, smile and have fun, with ideas coming from the children themselves. Surely, one or two ideas will help you start your curriculum content in a natural, effortless way. I ask each 'provoking' question with special mime and intonation. Whispering has the best effect, and lowering my head below the eye level of the children. This way, children will be attentive, interested and intrigued by what might happen next. Another very helpful tactic is to introduce a mystery bag containing diverse tiny things: a cotton ball, a rock, a leaf etc. The presence of the material, the palpable and the visible, will make children be even more intrigued.

How else can we add wonder to our teaching?

We all know that children love patterns, rituals and repetition. All of these actions confer feelings of security, self-confidence, independence and safety to all children. Knowing what is next offers the power to take the next step without fear. Children are motivated by resolving regular, logical patterns: they love to look forward to what is predictable.

Teachers can introduce the unexpected without taking away feelings of safety, so important for children. Adding unpredictable wonder to an expected flow of action will do this for us. So how is it done?

For a theme on the Senses, I started by trying to come up with an imaginary character who would come with us into the unknown world of the senses. I looked around the office and found a piece of cloth and a square small box. I wrapped the box in the cloth, I tied a ribbon under the box to form a 'neck' and there it was: a strange, square-headed being with absolutely no resemblance to a human. I took the being into the classroom and started my 'Magic Circle Time'.

The imaginative 'game' asked: 'I wonder, if you looked out of your window one day, and there was somebody on your windowsill, who would you like it to be?' The question produced hundreds of scenarios and possible visitors. I just had to get into the game and tell them that last night this really happened in my dream: a strange somebody was sitting on my windowsill trying to tell me something. I didn't understand him at all because, just imagine it, he had no mouth, no ears, no nose and no eyes!! At this moment 'wonder' is introduced into the lesson and children will not want to let it go. The week passed with the expected addition of the mouth, eyes, ears and nose of 'ASI' (the name the children gave my character). Even if children knew what was coming (expected completion of the pattern), the wonder of the topic was never lost. Weeks after the end of the Senses theme, ASI sat on a cupboard, looking down at us. Children continued to talk to him.

Now it is time for 'magic' to come into the picture: the magical powers of children to adapt to the real world around them, with the help of their own familiar world, and the magical powers of teachers to enter the worlds of children and learn their language.

Magic

Magic is the power to change the world around you.
Magic is the advantage of childhood over adulthood.
Magic is everything that does not exist.
Magic is the secret language of childhood.

Magic is always present in my teaching. I talk naturally about magical things. Speaking to children about ASI or with ASI is always as natural as talking to another person. Children do 'know' the difference between reality and fantasy, but they openly express the need for magic, the need for conquering the impossible. They accept magic as part of their development, as part of their mission. Magic can consist of certain looks, gestures or intonations. It can be a darkened room, a special candle, a mysterious sound, a relaxing melody or just a special atmosphere. Magic is there to create a more natural and relaxed channel of communication between children and adults. Magic is a universal language.

Each teacher can access magic. We have all been children, we have all been in love with the imaginary characters of our childhood and we have all constructed an imaginary world that revolved around an axis that we have drawn. Why not access again the latent powers within us and use them as teaching tools? These powers and ways of understanding will manage to guide us into the world of children and they will also lead us toward accessible and understandable curriculum content.

Why not have an adventurous '2' who escapes from our maths poster one day? He just decided to leave all the other numbers and try his luck alone in the world. Start the day by leaving the children to discover the missing number, have a group discussion about what has happened. Ask questions like:

- 'What should we do now?'
- 'How do you think "2" is feeling now?'
- 'How can we help him in his quest?'
- 'Do you think he is missing us?'

Start a 'search' for '2', asking the children to remember what he looks like. Ask them to draw a map for themselves and write a '2' on the map so they won't forget what he looks like. Even your dreamer child from the group will learn what a '2' looks like!

This whole event can be created by simply cutting out the '2' one day from your maths poster. Isn't that magic?

Lessons like this feel like play. Children feel secure in the tasks you give and they are excited by them, loving every moment of the magical trip to knowledge. Children need magic and imagination. Organising the search for the missing-alive number will provide you joy and excitement, as well. You will participate together with your children as they propose scenarios and predict outcomes.

Teachers are not merely the tools of communication between the curriculum and children, artificial funnels that shrink the world's information and pour it into children. The traditional ways of teaching young children are based on psychological studies and research that have tried to define and decode the mystery that is 'children'. I believe that all children have the right to be an un-decoded mystery, and teachers and parents should not try to crack the combination.

In my teaching, I never forget what breathtaking powers children have and how complex they are. They make sense of the real world around them. They translate information from their environment into their own 'language' with their own capacities of understanding. This is why it seems difficult to comprehend certain symbols transmitted by children to us, teachers, or to find a clear relation to a certain subject of discussion. We should never stay detached when a moment like this occurs. Children always have a meaning behind their statements.

Often we are trying too hard with our logic, and we forget that we can magically enter the children's world, just by using our hearts. If all teachers began by looking inside themselves, and searching for their own connection to the topic, learning would take place in a much better way. Adding emotion to the curriculum is a step toward successful teaching. If we are lucky, we can all recall teachers who taught us things we have never forgotten – because they were not afraid to open up to their students.

Teachers represent the real value of the educational process. As long as teachers keep *wonder and magic* as omnipresent constituents of teaching, children will feel *welcome* to learning. Add my three words to the fence of your teaching world and enjoy the ride.

Take a tip

Adopt an affective curriculum and try out the following exercise.

If you wish, play a game with me right now. Please write down three of your earliest memories. When you are done (I am positive that during this exercise you have smiled or had a sad expression on your face), please attach to each of your memories a list of the emotions you felt while remembering them or during your short time travel. The emotions you have collected now are the affective instruments your memories cling to. If everything you were taught in school had involved these emotions, you would have remembered considerably more details than otherwise.

Reading and resources

Cant A. (1999) 'Using fantasy to enhance young children's development and education', Vancouver: Master's thesis, Simon Fraser University.

Carson, R. (1998) *The Sense of Wonder*, New York: HarperCollins.

Egan, K. (1997) *The Educated Mind* (Introduction), Chicago, IL: University of Chicago Press.

——(ed.) (2007) *Teaching and Learning outside the Box: inspiring imagination across the curriculum*, London Ontario: Althouse Press.

——(2008) PowerPoint presentation at *Open Eyes Conference on Imaginative Education*, Cluj/Napoca, October.

Making time and space

Dancing on the decking

Rose observes: 'The boys had time and space to be creative in a dance conversation'

Outside on the decking, on a warm spring day, an adult had prepared bowls of water with big decorating paint brushes and a CD player, in the expectation that children would 'paint' with the water on the decking or the walls. The music was an experiment to observe whether it impacted on the children's response or not. Lots of children were quickly drawn to the area and began painting with the water, mainly around the edges of the decking area. As soon as the adult put the music on, two boys began to dance in the middle of the area while the other children painted around them. The boys moved rhythmically, with their dances flowing together. Sometimes, one of the boys would reflect the other boy's dance in his own movements, and sometimes the other way round. One would fall to the ground and then the other would move around him and dance away, and then fall himself. Then one would twirl around on his bottom and stand up again. The other boy would respond with a similar sequence of moves at the other end of the decking, and then they would spontaneously move towards each other and pass each other as they changed places. Their dances wove in and out of each other's. They appeared aware of each other, but also very self-absorbed in their own movements. They interpreted the music and changed pace with the tempo. Their movements were rhythmical throughout, as they twirled and stepped and leapt. They continued to dance in the centre of the decking, using all the available space, while other children painted with water around them. They smiled throughout and there was a certain humour in their dance. It continued for twenty minutes. The dance was delightful. At times it seemed almost choreographed, especially in the way in which their individual movements seemed linked. There was no talk, but non-verbal communication between them, and certainly an awareness of each other. They appeared exhilarated by their dance, but never overexcited.

Rose's favourite story books for children in her nursery class

Adams, G. (1994) *Flapjack and Waddle*, London: Orion Children's.

Butterworth, N. (1997) *The Treasure Hunt*, London: Picture Lions.

Hutchins, P. (1975) *Goodnight Owl*, London: Puffin Books

Listening more and talking less

Nurturing children's creativity

Kay Rooks

It was 8.45 a.m. early in September 1986 and the room was ready for the nursery children to arrive. I stood back to view the creative area and check that all was prepared. Four tables were pushed together and covered with newspaper, held together with sellotape, to keep them still and clean. There was a piece of white A3 rectangular paper carefully placed at each corner of the table, and in the centre four pots of ready-mix paint: red, yellow, blue and green, each pot complete with brush. On another table there were four neat balls of play dough, four boards, four rolling pins and an assortment of cutters. Three tables were held together with sellotaped newspaper to create a junk modelling area, complete with four yoghurt pots of glue, four spreaders and an assortment of boxes and materials. The room was ready for children's creativity – or was it?

This room was the starting point for my journey as a teacher of young children. Writing about it has given me the chance to explore and confirm my belief that I have been given a wonderful opportunity to nurture young children's creativity by

- listening more and talking less;
- giving children time and space;
- standing back to observe more;
- documenting what children tell me, so we can revisit their learning.

My first year in the nursery classroom started a journey of discovery and learning for me. I had set myself a personal challenge, to discover whether children in the nursery classroom had as much, more or less opportunity to engage in meaningful conversation with adults as did the children in the reception class where I had taught for two years. This question developed from my professional study of language development at Durham University, where I had begun to read the work of Vivien Paley. Paley, an American kindergarten teacher, had successfully embarked upon annual studies of the learning and development of her classes of children, through setting classroom-based research questions. Paley was determined to become a better listener and to understand the children she worked with more deeply: 'In my early teaching years I was in the wrong forest, I paid scant attention to the play and did not hear the stories' (Paley 1991: 5).

I became increasingly fascinated by her descriptions of how she developed her ability to listen to and interact with the children. She would tape-record and then analyse the children's discussions, using her analyses to develop the children's social understanding, use of language and learning through narrative story telling. I followed in her footsteps, making a huge effort *to listen to the children more and talk less*, trying to understand their thinking and to encourage the development of their thoughts and ideas. During that first term, I learned that, if I took time to listen to children during their activities, and began to use a few well-chosen words, I could provide opportunities for children to talk more and could extend their ideas and thoughts through offering thoughtful suggestions and provocations. Within the Early Years Foundation Stage framework (DFES 2007) this is referred to as engaging in 'sustained shared thinking'. All spaces within the learning environment, indoors and outdoors, were spaces for communication, but my focus of interest was drawn to the creative areas. I became fascinated with the stories behind children's creativity as they described their thoughts, feelings and ideas, and I began to realise that the finished painting, model or structure did not provide enough information, that I needed to learn more about the process leading to the creation.

I had always viewed the creative spaces as places for production, where children would produce a picture or a model with the materials I provided for them. I will use the art table as an example. At my starting point in September 1986, I thought that children would visit the art table themselves or through my direction and would work alone to create their pictures. The piece of white rectangular paper, four pots of coloured paint and brushes would stimulate their creative processes, and each child would complete their work in one attempt, spending approximately five to ten minutes to complete a picture. Through my conversations and observations, I began to realise that children often chose to collaborate with others – either another child or an adult – to produce their pictures. Although I had only provided four colours, the children were capable of pretending that brown and orange were really there, informing me that their Mum had brown hair or their tiger was orange, as they worked. I began to see that children often reached a point in their work where they wanted to leave it and return later, or that they wanted to add another section or change something during a return visit, developing the skill of redrafting. I can compare this to my own work: how many times have I revisited this chapter to reword and edit my writing? If I had written it in just one draft over a finite piece of time, it would look very different.

Taking time to listen to the children and offer comments and suggestions, I began to become more interested in the process of their work and the language they used to explain that process. Whereas in the beginning I might have accepted the red blob in the centre of the page as a red blob and said, 'What a lovely picture! Now pop it to dry', or attempted to make sense of what I saw with a comment like, 'That's a nice red blob! Is it an egg?' I became fascinated to know how the red blob had appeared and what the child had created. I needed to develop my listening and questioning skills considerably, so that I was demonstrating genuine interest and support in the child's learning processes.

> Creativity becomes more visible when adults try to be more attentive to the cognitive processes of children than to the results they achieve in the various fields of doing and understanding.
>
> (Malaguzzi in Edwards et al. 1998: 77)

Over the next few years I stretched my own boundaries by developing the art table to offer more flexible choices for children and by allowing greater freedom around time and space. Children were given permission to revisit their creative works and could spend time deliberating, redrafting or simply starting again.

When I moved to become a teacher in a nursery school I was able to develop a much deeper understanding of learning and teaching and of the complex nature of creativity. I had begun to question the products that children were expected to produce, conveniently labelled as artwork. The mass-produced identical Christmas cards, calendars and table decorations proved a huge challenge to my conscience, as did the conventional wall friezes of scrunched-up tissue paper-filled outlines and cardboard cut-out flowers and trees. Although these activities may have a place somewhere in the child's learning, they cannot be classed as the creativity of the child, only the creativity of the adult who possessed the thought and developed it into reality.

I embarked upon a more individualised route to Christmas creativity. Each child in my teaching group, twenty children in all, designed and made their own Christmas card and message. We had long discussions about the card possibilities, from colour and shape to design, and we spent time looking at Christmas cards and wrapping paper for ideas. Every child chose a different theme, ranging from camels to Santa Claus, and they chose lots of different media to work with, from glue and glitter to felt and pipe cleaners. I cannot say that the sessions were not sometimes a little frantic, that there were not accidents and mistakes, and sometimes children needed to rethink or compromise their ideas, with support and encouragement from me, but the rewards of their endeavours came on the last day of term when the children took their Christmas cards home. As I stood at the exit door, I observed each child tell their parent the story of their Christmas card and why it was special to them.

One reason for my deepening knowledge and understanding of children's learning during my teaching time at the nursery was my opportunity to develop enhanced *observation* skills. The nursery school practitioners were in the process of developing a system for observing children and their play opportunities in the workshop areas, indoors and outdoors. A powerful motivating force in this work was the language development of children, one of the main aims of the nursery being to enhance the children's vocabulary development and language skills. The practitioners had studied the work of Joan Tough in order to support their understanding of children's language development and the role of the adult in fostering it. Joan Tough purposely uses the word 'fostering' as it indicates that the adult must be aware of children's language development and promote appropriate experiences to allow it, through the children's immediate interests.

> The child's interests and curiosity will motivate him to communicate and so he will use language to generate his own ideas and then to express them. He will begin to take an active part in promoting his own skill of thinking.
>
> (Tough 1980: 4)

The practitioners became skilled in deciding whether a child was reporting, reasoning, predicting, imagining or projecting, and whether a child could ask questions as well as answer them. They understood how to ask real, curious questions to sustain the conversation and to discover what a child was truly thinking and imagining.

CHILD: I can see the sun and I can see the moon. That's not right is it?
ADULT: Why do you think that?

CHILD: There should just be one.
ADULT: I wonder what has happened?
CHILD: I think the sun is saying 'good night' to the moon.

As practitioners observed children and their play opportunities, they wrote down what they saw and heard. They were careful to include not only what the children said but also their communications through different mediums, such as art or music or non-verbal gesture.

Linked to the observations, we had regular discussions about the children's learning and what we could do to extend this further. For example, when a group of children showed an interest in pirates, we discussed how we could develop their interest further. We looked for 'provocations' to stimulate further learning: pirate books and pictures to stimulate talk, pirate accessories to add to the role-play and outdoor areas and small-world characters and resources for the construction space. Through the children's interests we could introduce writing, reading, number and/or creative opportunities. These discussions were a wonderful opportunity to discuss ideas, thoughts and dilemmas about children's learning and our teaching. All contributions were valued and we learned from each other, using our strengths to form a collegiate team.

Much later I learned that this listening, watching, observing, discussing and documenting are part of a daily routine for the practitioners at Reggio Emilia in Italy. It was not until 2006 that I had the chance to visit.

Visiting Reggio Emilia

One of my desires during my visit to Reggio Emilia was to discover more about the *projects* and *documentation* that the Italians have striven to perfect over many years. I had read about their philosophy of learning and teaching and the processes teachers, *pedagogistas* and artists employ to support children's learning. I knew how much they valued *time* and *space* for creative learning. I learned that the creation of appropriate spaces for children – not the number of adults employed – was vital if children were to create, imagine, discuss and interact. I saw their philosophy in practice in their pre-schools and remember especially the inspiring examples I witnessed there.

As we arrived in Italy we were informed that spring had just arrived. The trees were in blossom and the days were warm and sunny. At one pre-school I visited, the children had found a toad in the outdoor play area and had placed it in a glass case in the indoor space to observe and study for a few days. The children had sought information about toads by searching the internet and reference books, and the practitioners had invited one parent, a zoologist, to visit the school to share his knowledge.

Two 5-year-old boys had been inspired by their new-found knowledge and decided to make a 'dragon toad' from clay. When I arrived for my visit to the school I watched these two boys as they talked and worked together on their creation. The toad was approximately two feet in height, with the obvious markings of a toad cut into the shape. However, the boys had allowed their imaginative ideas to take shape, for this toad was half fantasy. It possessed the features of a dragon, with a long spiked tail, and two large horns protruding from the head. At that point they were engrossed in the tail and they concentrated on how to shape and form it. They saw me watching and eventually began to explain their work to me. Although I speak no Italian I could understand from gesture their excitement about the features of their toad. They found it highly amusing that I could not speak their language, but continued to show me their work.

I sought out the teacher, who explained that these two boys had chosen to work on their dragon toad every day for the last two weeks, although the spent time varied each day. It was accepted that this piece of work might take a long time to complete and that the children were under no pressure to finish their creation within a certain time frame. The unfinished toad was left in the art workshop area, or atelier, for the two boys to revisit whenever they wished. No child or adult interfered with the 'dragon toad' creation, demonstrating to me that children's work is taken seriously and shown the respect it deserves.

I watched two girls, aged approximately 4 years, as they spent at least twenty minutes interacting at a piece of shared artwork. The large rectangular canvas was attached to a wall and the watercolour brushes and paints were in an attached tray below. The canvas was well covered with a variety of blue spirals when I arrived at the scene, and the two girls were busy finding spaces to add further spirals. They shared space and resources and drew each spiral with great care and attention to detail, each shape taking a few minutes to complete. The spirals were different sizes and different shades of blue and although I could not understand their language, I watched the girls' exchanges, gestures and movements as they shared in the experience together. They compared shades, discussed where each spiral should be placed and provided support and challenge to each other. Throughout this activity no adult was present, but it was obvious that these children were learning.

I saw what educators in Reggio Emilia mean when they speak of children reading their own and each other's *drawings*, seeing visual representations as *graphic languages* (Edwards, Gandini and Forman 1998: 34). When the Reggio Emilia children are involved in collaborative projects, their responses to exploratory experiments with materials involve several such languages at once:

> Word, gesture and mental image were the three mutually nurturing elements of an indissoluble relationship. Words followed gestures, which followed words, which followed images, which followed gestures, which followed words.
>
> (Vecchi and Giudici 2004: 30)

My visit to Italy also provided me with the opportunity to reflect on many aspects of learning and teaching linked to creativity, and in particular I was inspired to consider the role of the artist in the pre-school environment.

The role of the artist

Within the last ten years my role has moved from being a classroom practitioner to supporting the practitioners who work with the youngest children, from birth to five years. I managed to secure some funding from the local authority to engage in a project organised by Sightlines Initiative, an organisation founded by Robin Duckett in Newcastle-upon-Tyne to encourage creative projects between practitioners, children and artists. Three schools volunteered to become involved in the project, and each school was introduced to an artist who developed a special relationship with the children and practitioners. Each project developed slightly differently in content, due to the interests of the children and the provocations that the adults, both practitioners and artists, provided following their observations and discussions each week. A mentor and an early years consultant also supported aspects of the project by helping with the documentation and taking photographs.

A conference was held at the end of the project to celebrate the achievements of the three schools and make the learning visible, and artists and practitioners took the floor to lead joint presentations of their individual projects. There was the story of the rainbows, which proved to be a riot of colour. Children were given the opportunity to explore and experiment with light, shadow and colour, create colourful patterns and construct three-dimensional rainbows. There was the wonderful alien adventure, which started from creating lands and islands with natural materials and led to children, practitioners and artist embarking upon a journey to outer space and the creation of a magnificent space rocket from canes and twigs. Finally, there was the marvellous mud adventure, in which the majority of children in the group wanted to explore the properties of mud, search in the mud and, eventually, experiment with jumping over the mud. The mud group work developed into a pirate adventure and the creation of a pirate ship from large cardboard boxes. One child chose a completely different path, for after finding a small bone in the mud, she became convinced that there were dinosaurs underground and spent her time searching for further bones, explaining where the dinosaurs had come from and discussing with the adults how she would nurture and care for any dinosaurs she might find.

Watching and listening as the presentations described the development of these projects, I realised that for the children, practitioners and artists this had been a huge learning journey of discovery, about learning, teaching and imaginative creativity. It had involved a huge step in risk-taking for the practitioners as they slowly let go of some of their control and observed children moving confidently into exploring their own interests. The PowerPoint presentations were the main products of the projects, for they contained the wonderful documentation of the children's learning as it unfolded week by week, and the photographs and recorded language of the children captured the essence of their thoughts, feelings and ideas.

An outdoor project for creative play

One element of my present role is providing support to nine nursery schools and one nursery head teacher who has embarked upon a similar journey with her own staff and children, as they considered developing their outdoor area as a place of creative play and exploration. The work was initially funded through a local authority project, with significant contribution from the nursery school's own budget. As in the projects above, the head teacher had chosen to work with an environmental consultant and a photographer to capture the development of the project as it unfolded, so providing a record of the children's and practitioners' learning. My role has been to listen to the head teacher talk through her feelings and ideas and her next steps in the development of the work.

The research question for the project was 'how do we enrich the outdoor environment?' The head teacher, practitioners and consultants spent a development day at the Rising Sun Country Park in North Tyneside, where they had the opportunity to audit the outdoor area and consider how it was being used by the staff and children, consider practitioners' likes, concerns and perceptions of working in the outdoors and evaluate the use of natural materials as inspirations for learning projects. The practitioners were already accustomed to reflective practice, documenting children's learning, and had recently completed an adaptation to the indoor environment, so the process was familiar to them.

The practitioners used a variety of methods to discover what the children were doing outside, including photographic maps, photographs of children's learning, introducing new materials, and open-ended questioning. It became clear that the children had found their own spaces for creative play – in the space between the fence and the shed, the bushes in the secret garden and the hedgerow at the perimeter fence. It was here that the children encountered monsters, dinosaurs and dragons.

Similar to the practitioners in my previous local authority, the practitioners saw the project as an opportunity for 'letting go', taking risks and being more adventurous, but were nervous of the prospect. The consultants were able to support the practitioners and record their feelings and thoughts during their weekly joint discussions. They took the opportunities that emerged through the children's interests, and one such interest that developed was the fire project, which lasted approximately two weeks. The introduction of a large log had led to the children pretending to make campfires and cooking imaginary food. Small-group time was used to explore this idea further and a group of children chose to pursue it, and sought out a suitable campfire site, eventually agreeing a space in the enclosed nature garden. Materials were gathered for a real fire, and one day it was decided to cook some real food. The learning experience included setting the rules for making and using the fire, and using the senses of smell, touch and taste, and the practitioners were able to document the learning.

The project has supported the practitioners in listening to the children's interests and supporting the development of learning through these interests, rather than planning rigidly. Documenting the learning has become of huge importance to the practitioners, who have come to realise that each one of them has differing documentation styles, and that it is difficult making decisions about what is significant to record. The use of photography has been crucial in capturing the children's learning experiences and the head teacher is keen to continue the work, because the journey is not yet complete.

Nor is my own learning journey finished, as I am still striving to learn more about learning and teaching the youngest age group of children, in the hope of sharing that with the practitioners I support. I have travelled far from those days long ago when I stretched my own boundaries as a practitioner and allowed children to mix their own paint, choose their own materials, leave unfinished work for days and weeks, and admit that I was uncertain what the children's outcome or products would be.

On my journey, I have been fortunate to work with children and adults who have challenged and supported my growth and development as a practitioner and I will strive to support and guide others.

> The gifted teacher is shaped not only by working together with children and other adults, but also by building together, making mistakes together, correcting, revisiting and reflecting on work that has to be done.
>
> (Malaguzzi in Edwards et al. 1998: 13)

Rose observes

A cabbage in an egg pot

Lee often spends an hour or more creating with glue, tape, scrap materials and paint every day that he is in nursery. Some time ago he spent his time making box models and wrapping each one up as a present. He would make one for Mummy, one for Daddy and one for his cat. More recently he found a strip of red paper and stuck it diagonally across a piece of paper, saying that this says 'No rubbish'. I asked him if he would like me to write his words on a post-it note to stick on his sign. He was pleased with this idea. Later that morning he painted a picture of a person and then he began to paint over the person. I sat nearby watching him paint and he said, 'The boy's hiding behind the curtain'. He asked me to write this down and he stuck the note in a corner where he hadn't painted. Later still he found me again, and asked if I could write 'A cabbage in an egg pot'. This time I was perplexed and went to look at the creation. He had taken the top of an egg box and crumpled a piece of red cellophane and stuck it inside the egg box lid. It was indeed a red cabbage in an egg box! Throughout the week he continued to find me to ask me to write notes for his creations. True, he was becoming aware of print and how his words could be written down and read later by his parents, but I felt this discovery also extended the creative process beyond the making of the models and paintings, to include his stories about them. It seemed crucial to him not only to tell an adult those stories but to see them written down.

Rose observes themes running through the play of children together

The Troll's house and the Empire State Building

Ben and his Mum had made a model of his house using boxes and yoghurt pots. There was a post-it note from her on the model explaining that Ben had added an extension in the shape of a tower which was the Troll's house and was purely imaginary. Ben and I talked about his house and he explained where everyone's bedrooms were. Then I asked about the tower and whether it was real or imaginary. 'Imaginary,' he said, and laughed. We placed the model on the display with other models.

The next day I saw Ben and his best friend playing in the block area with his model. They had placed the model on the carpet and surrounded it with cylindrical blocks – large cylinders standing upright, with smaller cylinders lying across the top of these. They told me it was a chocolate factory and the cylinders were the chocolates. Ben pointed at the Troll's house saying,

> *'This is the customer place.'*
> *'Oh,' I said. 'Where the customers can buy chocolates?'*
> *Ben answered. 'Yes. It's the shop!'*

That afternoon, Ben joined a group in the block area again. We were looking at architects' drawings and photographs of buildings. Some children were interested in the architects' plans and began drawing their own plans using paper on clipboards. Ben fetched his model again and drew it, using one piece of paper for his house and another for the Troll's house. He looked carefully at the detail in his model and represented it clearly in his drawings. He then asked me to label the drawings, telling me what to write, and then he connected the written words by drawing arrows to the corresponding parts of the building.

After this he continued playing in the area with a younger girl. They looked at a large poster of the skyline of New York and created the Empire State Building, looking closely at the detail in the photograph and using different sets of blocks to recreate it accurately.

This creative conversation spanned two days but also built on the established relationship between Ben and me. He often shares his ideas with me and we talk about what he is creating. Here, he was able to make links in his learning between home and nursery through the activity at home and the dialogue his Mum had initiated with the post-it note. His Mum had nurtured his creativity by allowing the extension in the form of an imaginary Troll's house, recognising the importance of his imaginary ideas. Ben enjoys exploring the meaning and sounds of new words and clearly liked the idea of the word 'imaginary'. Later Ben's model provided a prop for more creative play when it became a chocolate factory. I loved the confidence he had that he could take his model from the display and use it in a playful context, and then later grasp the idea of drawing it when he observed other children thinking about drawing plans or diagrams of their block models. The dialogue between us continued as he recognised the potential of using written words to label his pictures.

Ben's play with Rita was delightful. I had not observed these two children playing together before. That they did so on this occasion illustrates how children playing alongside each other seem to recognise a shared interest and how their play begins to flow into each other's as they develop the narrative. Rita is quieter and younger than Ben but they built together as equal partners, incorporating each other's ideas and referring back to the photograph to guide them. Rita has an older brother and I felt that she was very comfortable playing with Ben, and he was also very responsive to her ideas.

Through the dialogue between adults and other children Ben explored and reflected on his creative ideas.

Take a tip

Reorganise your creativity area as a resource base. This allows children to experiment with colour mixing so that they can make orange if they need it for their painting of a tiger, or of ginger hair. They may need different-sized brushes to suit their purposes. They need to find out the various properties of materials, what can be done with glue and paint and clay, often with your help.

Reading and resources

DFES (Department for Education and Skills) (2007) *The Early Years Foundation Stage: setting the standards for learning, development, and care from birth to five*, London: Department for Education and Skills, www.teachernet.gov.uk/publications.

Edwards, C., Gandini, L. and Forman, G. (1998) *The Hundred Languages of Children, the Reggio Emilia Approach – Advanced Reflections*, London: JAI Press Ltd.

Moss, P. (2004) 'Children in Europe; celebrating 40 years of Reggio Emilia', *Children in Europe*, 6 (March).

Paley, V. (1991) *The Boy Who Would Be A Helicopter*, Cambridge, MA and London: Harvard University Press.

Tough, J. (1980) *Talking and Learning*, Glasgow and London: Wardlock Educational.

Vecchi, V. and Giudici, C. (2004) *Children, Art, Artists: the expressive languages of children, the artistic language of Alberto Burri*, Reggio Emilia: Reggio Children.

3 Enriched environments

A dialogue with people, places and materials

Fleur Griffiths in conversation with Tracy Kirkbride

Children interact with people, places and materials and slight changes act as a *provocation* for new exploration and enquiry. This was exemplified for me in a video taken in a Reggio pre-school or *nido* (nest). It shows how the environment is arranged to provoke learning, seen as an interactive and creative process. This is captured in my diary entry:

> Small pieces of clay provoked rolling, squeezing, poking, pressing into shape – the grammar of gesture – as small children made meaning: a snake, a tree, a ball. Placing these on a communal board, the children called others to come and see their creations. Slowly a story develops between the elements. One child wants to play outside but she does not simply run off; she passes on the story in words and gestures to a friend who continues the ever-evolving story.
>
> By contrast, enormous blocks of clay provoke a different response: climbing, balancing, indenting hand- and footprints into the soft surface. The children help each other move up and down. One child draws attention by gesture to the way he can mount a horse which he pretends to feed with grass. Others latch on to the idea and ride their horses. Here starts a dialogue between children and materials and an imaginative social engagement between children too young to speak.

The educator notices these exchanges and tries to document them with photos or video. This provides evidence to be shared and interpreted by teacher, artist, *pedagogista*, building their particular perspectives into a possible explanation – a suggested significance in these actions. Such visible evidence can then create a memory, shared by child, parent and educators. It can also suggest the next step or provocative extension. The children need the adults to listen to these many languages and give them voice.

Here is a clear example of Reggio's philosophy in practice. Children in play communicate creatively and the adults respect and trust that, given the right spur, children together will learn. Adults will try to build on what the children, by their actions, are telling them. They will discuss together possible significances and ways forward. They are aware that there are *grammars* in all meaning-making communications, not just the verbal ones. As with speech, children need the opportunities to explore what can be *said* by the many languages available to them, in this case by gesture, manipulation, movement and socio-dramatic play. Children want to explore materials, like clay or glue or pastel, to discover what can be done with them. Adults need to allow children the chance to develop all these creative avenues of communication.

No one understands this better than Tracy Kirkbride, one of the collaborators for this book. She has taken this vision of learning and teaching and applied it in her school, being aware of the curbs that different cultures impose. When she joined in our discussion about what creativity meant in her context, she recounted the Jam Jar project. She refers to the photos that document the visible and sharable evidence of the *deep* learning that took place. As she talks, Tracy turns the pages of a picture book which document the development of a project initiated by one child and leading to the involvement and extended learning of the whole class over a period of time.

The Jam Jar project

I have brought along a series of photographs from what I would call a project that evolved from a child's interest, from one boy's interest and that interest was – jam jars! Now the jam jars were used intentionally by the adults to house paintbrushes, not to be used for music. However, he took the jam jars, emptied out the brushes and put them all on the floor. Now I was working with play dough at the time, the malleable area, and I just watched as this took place: one jar was there, and then another and then there were lots. I didn't say anything as I just wanted to see how it evolved; by my questioning or by saying anything about what he was doing I would stop him, so I carried on playing with these children here. Then he went to the malleable area and started playing with the wooden spoons, tapping with them, and he started just to experiment with the sound that was taking place. Then he went to get some smaller jars and started to hit those, and still I didn't say anything. Then a little girl who was playing over at the other side came over to watch. She didn't say anything to the little boy, but started to do the same thing as him – just hitting the jars. Again I didn't go over and didn't question them. Then a few other children came along and joined in. This all happened in one session; it just evolved.

Then they went to other areas and got other things to hit. They seemed to like this action of just hitting. This went on for quite a long time, but I felt that it was important time because they were communicating with each other through actions, through the sounds that they were making. The boy who started it was actually further on than the other children because he was experimenting with smaller containers and larger ones. The others were just hitting the things that were on the carpet. After a period of time I joined them and I actually didn't say anything, but I started just to mirror the actions of the little boy who had started it. Then, as I did it more and more, more and more children joined me, and that was the most magical experience I've had for a long time. I felt each and every one of us, that is, my whole class, communicating without speaking, but we were communicating a sense of beat, of rhythm. I then started to beat a pattern and they replicated that pattern, but without speaking. We didn't say, 'Do it like this'.

I felt that I wanted to extend that learning a little bit more and take it on to another level, because the enthusiasm that was there was so strong. So what we did over a period of time, we played again, again on the carpet, but then introduced water: what would happen if we put water in those containers? … If we put water into the containers what would the sound be like? So we created high sounds and low sounds. The children joined in with that and they interpreted those high and low sounds in whatever way they wanted, and then they closed their eyes and they listened, and then they would tell me what kind of sound it was.

But that was not planned. The learning experience that came from that was of such high quality. We started to think about how else we could use the beat and that steady action, so we clapped. I didn't want to limit the children's interpretation of that, because some children wanted to use the beaters, some wanted to clap, but I knew that there would be other children who would have other ideas. We carried on facilitating this extension with the water, and the children just did it themselves and experimented with the sounds: what would happen if I filled the jar to the top; what would happen if it was not very full at all? Then we looked at drumming, drumming with lots of different materials: what could we use to make a sound with, really listen to the sounds?

Then – and this was after quite a long period of time – we invited some drummers in. The drummers didn't go into the hall and play for the children to listen. I didn't tell the children they were coming and they just walked through our setting and didn't say anything. The children looked and looked, quite perplexed – what on earth is happening? 'Miss Kirkbride, you didn't tell us!' The drummers were just walking through and playing this beat. So then this little boy – the one who had started it – followed him and the man who had started the drumming sat down in the outdoor area and the little boy got a piece of construction material and started to drum it. Then some other boys copied and they started to play the wooden bricks. Then some girls started playing on the metal posts, but they had metal spoons – they had previously used these spoons to beat on metal. Then some other children joined and danced; they danced around just however they wanted to respond to the music. And another man came with his drum and started playing. Then I and another teacher came outside and my instant reaction was to dance, and I *wanted* to dance. I didn't want to play. I just wanted to dance, so I danced!

The whole class, and I know it sounds idealistic, joined in the session, every single one of them interpreting the beat in their own way, through their own gut reactions – not through what the teacher was telling them to do. They had the confidence that had been built up through this and other reactive projects, which enabled them to react in this way, because they didn't have the prescriptive curriculum that tells them: 'This is what you do when this happens'. For me, that session is the most inspirational session I have ever experienced. The outdoor area is an uninhibited area – not structured by classroom – that's very open and allowed them the freedom to respond in their own way. We were not saying this is the convention, this is a four-walled classroom – it was happening outside. They used the knowledge they had got along their journey to interpret that music on that day. They were *ready* to take on that learning experience.

What was striking about this account was the *trust* that Tracy showed in her children to find a way of discovering answers for themselves. She knew when to stand back and when to join the play and provoke extensions to their learning. She had confidence that she was co-constructing significant meanings with the children. She based her confidence on the build-up over time of the shared values of respect and participation.

I took up the theme of *trust* when I visited her school, and we taped our conversation.

Tracy is happy that the transcript reflects what she most keenly wished to convey about her vision of teaching and learning. Readers will miss out on her other, unspoken languages – her gestures, emphases, differing pace and changing moods, from excitement to reflective calm. Perhaps a video could capture such messages more fully. This is why camera and tape/video recorder are such important tools for helping to make meaning visible.

Tracy talks to Fleur about her creative classroom, both indoors and out

FLEUR: In our group you were talking about trust and you said that your children trust in the environment. The environment is their responsibility as well as your responsibility. Can you explain this?

TRACY: Yes, the trust comes in so powerfully. For the trust to be there, it requires so many elements and the environment is a key part of it. The way the environment is set up is determined by the children. The way they communicate about the environment is by their actions, not by their words. Children of 4 and 5 years old will not tell you that they don't like an area, but the use they make of it tells us what they value. If they don't like an area, they neglect it or ignore it.

For example, we felt that we were neglecting an element of construction, and we needed to think how we could incorporate building inside the classroom (I don't like the word any more) because there was such an interest being shown in fixing things together outside, and we thought we could bring that inside. Initially, after school, the staff set up a big tray in the space indoors with baskets of materials around. When the children came in, they were excited at first by the new area. They noticed a change.

They couldn't say exactly what was different but they reacted by moving the tray right out of the space and the baskets as well! What they were telling us was that the space was too cluttered. They were saying in their heads, 'What do you expect me to do here? You are overloading me with far too many materials. I don't need all these materials. I will tell you what I need by getting what I want. I don't need all this equipment. I'll show you by my actions what I need. I can get it myself. I don't need it laid out in front of me.'

What we want to bring out in children is this independence: 'I can find what I need; I might have to go outside to find it or to another area, but I shall find it. You don't need to put it under my face, to tell me how to use it.'

FLEUR: So you want more clear spaces and you've been in a fight against clutter and too much busyness in the environment.

TRACY: Yes, yes. Many years ago, my practice consisted of labelling equipment boxes and overloading environments by giving children too much choice. That choice was not related to their interests and because of that, much of the equipment was not used. So, by tighter planning, team planning, coming together every day and evaluating the learning we've observed, as adults and children together, we have decluttered our rooms. Then we feel our learning opportunities are right and the children feel they are right – until the children tell us otherwise through communication of actions, not through words. And that is through tight observation – observation needs to happen all the time. Those spontaneous things that we see, those are noted. Adults are constantly watching children. We don't need to say 'Today we are going to focus on communication, language and literacy and we are going to look at how someone writes a sentence.' That is far too structured for our environment. We observe what the children are doing at the time and we would not lead learning that was not happening at that time. And that's why our observations lead us to better learning, because we take the children from where they are to where they want to go. Take writing, for example. Writing is fantastic in our class, not because we sit at the front and teach it but because we provide, in our environment, the equipment children are asking for to serve their writing purposes. They have reason to write, and they are wanting to practise it and adults are here as facilitators, as scaffolders and as people who can extend them. They will ask us for that. We don't have to interfere in their learning. They will invite us in to their learning. So, our standards (and I don't like that word either) are very high, through children telling us what they want, through their actions and through the environment facilitating that learning. So, all of those things come together: the role of the adult; the role of observation which is key to getting the environment right.

We plan and evaluate with the children; that is not separate; we are not seen as apart. We ask the children all the time, and then we have a period of reflection – the children know it is time to think about what is working. So, although the children have been communicating through their actions all week, we now share with them what we have seen and we acknowledge their learning, and they are clear where they are going next.

FLEUR: And you are now giving them the words.

TRACY: Yes, we give them words. They sometimes find it hard to articulate the meaning of what they are doing, but by our interpreting that – and obviously we want the children to tell us when we are wrong – and giving recognition to that, and by having review time with the children, yes, we are giving them the words. But we are also leading their learning on through where they are telling us to go.

FLEUR: This is a kind of conversation isn't it? You as an adult are watching, listening so closely to what is on the child's mind, and following that lead.

TRACY: Absolutely. We give recognition to that by having a board for planning. The children then see the value of that. The board has photos of key learning opportunities we've captured and we analyse that with the children. We then add the children's words, typed up, and tell them what's there. We share: 'This is what we did and this is why we are doing this next.' This is the idea of carrying on learning: not learning that is separate, not separated learning areas, not separate subjects, but blended learning. Not saying, 'This is numeracy, this is literacy', because what significance does that have for any child?

FLEUR: Children are not in the compartments we seek to put them into. This is what is so striking to me, going round your school, that the categories of activity that used to determine the shape of nursery – sand there, construction there, water play there – do no longer apply. Instead, you are thinking more, 'What can children create, what sense can they make, given these spaces and access to these materials, and we'll see what they do. There's no limit to what they might use the spaces for.'

TRACY: It is about open-endedness. Open-endedness means we do not have that expectation that everyone will produce a near-identical model. We know that every child is different, so why should we have the same expectation for everyone? Each one has something to bring to this environment and we want to see it. If we do not allow opportunities to see it, we will never see it. We want children to succeed in education. We don't want them to fail. So we provide the open-endedness that allows them the forum to succeed. And to feel valued. Not to be put into boxes. And to feel we can achieve anything together.

FLEUR: It's the children's narratives that drive planning and they are not pre-set. So, if the snow comes, a snow house emerges, the polar bear appears, stories feed in and the theme carries the learning forward, would you say?

TRACY: Exactly. Again, through observation we pick up on children's interests. It might be a story that captures interest and the children, in their own time, develop it, maybe through writing or going to create something, a painting. Then they would bring this back to the group and tell the others what they have done and then someone else joins on. We can't NOT follow the children's interests. They are telling us in their own way how they want to learn. We have to listen and take that forward, and the environment evolves. The real experience of snow was the starting point and that linked into story. So it is real life linking in to story. I think children crave that real experience first so that they really know, if you see what I mean.

FLEUR: I do. I was trained in the 1960s so we would not have dreamed of doing anything else but starting with real sensory experience: the falling snow, the ladybird that flies in – you use what happens by chance. So, you have to be flexible and spontaneous.

Walking round your areas, I notice that there are transitional spaces, where clearly one idea is losing power and another idea is taking over.

TRACY: Absolutely. For instance, in this environment you can see the ideas of building, of fixing and joining are coming through. And the children are helping to frame this. They may bring things from outside, inside. The children are asking for it to happen in this way. They are starting to form their own spaces.

Like the idea of the dark area. They use this in many, many, different ways but a learning story that is in my room at the moment is of the disco. This happened spontaneously from an item that they found: as they placed it on the projector, they realised that it reflected light right across the ceiling. Obviously, this catches every child's attention and they all looked to see what was happening. Lots of children joined in at first and they shouted, 'Look, Miss Kirkbride, we're having a disco!' That was clearly an invitation into play, and we started to investigate how we could create more colour; what would happen if we put the colours directly into the light? We realised that this learning experience was very powerful and we could not ignore it. So, we observed it; took lots of photographs of it and with the children we told the story of that learning. It then became embedded in their minds and was powerful, and they recognised that we valued it by talking of the importance of it.

FLEUR: What I like is the fact that this builds up a sort of class culture that they all share in; it is not just celebrating the creativity of one person. It permeates throughout: one person has an idea and others catch on. One idea propels the next idea.

TRACY: Absolutely. Lots of learning journeys here have started from one child or two children, but because of the powerfulness of that learning, it has helped to draw in more children, and those children have taken on the learning opportunity which was originally for those two children. That says a lot for the powerfulness of that learning and the freedom allowed to children in this environment. By allowing children to pick up objects which you would never think could go together, new learning happens. The children are making planes at the moment and what they are decorating them with is fantastic. Things we would never imagine, especially if we are in the 'every model the same' culture and our imagination has become restricted. Children know in this kind of environment, that there are no limits to the possible. So the things they use are so obscure but look so fantastical, yet they can explain the significance of every single part of it and why they have used materials. How on earth could they do that if the materials weren't there? Or, if you were saying, 'No you can't go outside to collect it or you can't go over there to get it because you must keep everything in this area.'

FLEUR: How do you keep things in some kind of order?

TRACY: Right, we have resource bases. So we try and keep certain types of things together so the children would know where to find, for example, paints; they would know where to find different types of brushes; they would know where to find paper.

FLEUR: Tools, really.

TRACY: They would know where to find tools, yes, but those tools can be used anywhere in the environment to help move their learning forward. But we would certainly not have areas called, 'The writing area', 'The painting area' ... because by putting those labels on those areas we are really just hindering the learning that could take place. So, why should we as adults have a *right* to stop learning from happening? My philosophy of the adult's role is this: people who *extend* learning through the many opportunities provided.

FLEUR: Where do you position yourself? Do you hide away? Do you have a good viewing position? Do you engage with a few and keep an eye on the others?

TRACY: I am usually invited into play. So when the children talk about where they are going to go – they may be carrying on with a project, they may be going back to something they were working on the day before – so before I can even decide where to go, I am invited in. It might be, 'Miss Kirkbride, can we carry on making our train?' And so here I am. The other children go to their projects; they are very focused on what they want to do. It's this idea of *sustained thinking, sustained learning*.

FLEUR: From day to day. Too many things are ephemeral, they are lost ... Children know time is short so they don't give time to creating something more lasting ... But here, they can find their train in a certain place, half-made from yesterday, and this could absorb them for days or weeks or however long it takes.

TRACY: Absolutely, it's slower learning. If we said, 'Time up. End of session! Tidy up. It's finished', then again, the learning opportunities have been hindered. What we would be saying is, 'It does not matter what you have been doing because it is finished now. We are on to something else.' We have to value what is taking place and *naturally* that learning will come to an end when they want it to. But we must, as adults, as facilitators, in this environment, help the children to get as much out of that experience as possible. So that is through clever questioning, through introducing new materials, through framing their ideas without leading them ...

FLEUR: Through what in Reggio would be called *provocations*.

TRACY: Absolutely, yes, and I think by doing that, you are enabling children to feel proud, to feel valued and to feel challenged. And if people say to me that in early years you can't challenge, that's all wrong. We can provide many challenges through open-ended environments and through providing the right resources, through very, very thorough observations.

FLEUR: Do you think that in training staff to carry out this kind of learning journey, the hardest thing to get across is these ways of provoking, of questioning and challenging?

TRACY: Very hard. It's a very hard skill.

FLEUR: A core skill but hard to make clear.

TRACY: We have a clear vision which we are developing (and as a practitioner you can never say you have got there, because teaching/learning is always evolving over time) but a clear philosophy is coming through which centres on questioning skills. How do we move learning forward without telling children how to do it? We seek to find out from them in our planning time together and they will tell us what helped them to learn. How do we ask open-ended questions, how do we scaffold learning? And that move forward often comes when a new resource is introduced. And as adults working together in a close team, we can ask each other questions about how best to move forward, to have a better understanding and to confront tricky situations. We are not on our own, trying to make sense of everything. Alone, we couldn't follow all these key moments.

FLEUR: You said you used the camera and also tape-recorded and typed up conversations to help you recognise and follow up these key moments.

TRACY: We have our camera attached to us.

FLEUR: ...On the hip! (*They laugh at the cowboy idea that comes up*)

TRACY: Yes, and at planning time, thinking of the next step, we can show the children those images and they help us to make sense of it sometimes. We say we don't understand fully and they come up with something fantastical and you think 'Wow! I'd never have thought of that! But now I do!' So it is something about trusting in the children. Don't underestimate what children can really give you, especially in a group. Don't be so ignorant as to assume that we don't have to listen to children and can simply take ideas from books, activity ideas. That is to miss their intelligence. They are extremely intelligent; their ideas far exceed my ideas and I am amazed every single day with what they can come up with.

FLEUR: I agree. You can never be bored with children, because you can always be surprised by their ideas.

How do you manage to follow this path AND keep pace with the things you have to do – the curriculum for instance?

TRACY: We try to link in as much as possible – going back to the blended learning we talked of earlier – the children's interests with what they unfortunately HAVE to do. For example, phonics, which is statutory for children this age – my children love it. That is because we link it in to what the children are learning. For example, the Three Little Pigs at the moment are in the building theme, the **s**traw, the **s**ticks and **s**tones. Stories provide the phonics. Everything we do should have *purpose*, *significance* and *link* with their current learning interest. If learning is standing on its own, no one can see where it is coming from or attach any significance to it.

You would not teach a child in the home like that – it's not common sense! So it is about using our common sense and taking away the clutter in education; and thinking, 'Right, I need to do phonics. How am I going to do it? I am going to link it in to what I am going to do anyway.' I know what can be achieved through following their interests. Yes, we have adult-led sessions in which we would follow on learning which has been seen to be significant. We could enrich vocabulary in those times, but that would always be linked to what they were doing.

FLEUR: So your child-initiated journeys and your child investigations create your curriculum.

TRACY: Yes, that is the key. And I think that is the key to success. And if anyone were to come into this environment, they would see every child deeply engaged and that is because we have got the curriculum right. And the curriculum comes from where? It comes from the children.

FLEUR: I have noticed how often the physical dividers and the pathways within the environment are altered to allow new spaces for new opportunities – always evolving new patterns, according to what you learn by listening and watching children react.

TRACY: We don't have furniture there because it has to be there, but because the children are asking for it. In our environment, there are not a lot of tables because there is not a real need for them. If the children seek out a table to sit around, that is one thing, but where there is an alternative way of children working and learning together, we provide that opportunity. There may come a time when more tables and chairs are called for, but in the meantime we leave space and wait until the children show the need for them – not because we, as adults, favour the arrangement, thinking it would look nice with a shelf there or a table there. Always we are looking for learning opportunities, not for what looks 'pretty'.

FLEUR: What alerts you to a key moment? What makes you know you have seen something significant?

TRACY: That's because we are very clever! (*They both laugh at the audacity of saying so*) We are very well tuned in to observation and I'd like to think we are becoming very skilled at it. Even if we are very much engaged with the child or children we are working with, we are always looking around us.

FLEUR: ...With eyes in the back of your head!

TRACY: Absolutely. We are always looking for actions, listening to voices. Many times it is because the children have called us over, because they have felt that magic moment. And in the example of the Jam Jar project, it was because I was watching very closely from the Playdoh table and they wanted me then to join in because they were asking me for ideas, they were asking what they could use, so I joined in their investigation, not with words but with actions. So I was invited in to a magical learning opportunity and I did what they were doing, not changing but extending it. If we try to change things by questioning 'Why?' and being intrusive, then that 'why' moment of learning stops. And I think that would be very dangerous to push it. There is a magical moment hiding in every single environment and it is about the adults being skilful enough to bring those magical moments out. Sometimes we get it wrong and we miss opportunities. But when we get it right and we feel the magic moment, it will stay with us for the rest of our lives.

FLEUR: ...Those moments of concentration which are often very quiet ones. You have said that your nursery is characterised by quiet absorption.

TRACY: ...Engagement, because the curriculum is right. I don't like the word curriculum, but let's say – 'The child-curriculum' is right because it reflects their interests. And their persistence to carry on, to concentrate, to succeed is because they have framed the learning opportunity themselves. We're there to provide and extend it. So, learning goes on as long as it possibly can and transforms. It doesn't stop, it endlessly transforms.

FLEUR: The question I feel many will ask is how you control – or better, how you oversee – so many different children, all wanting to be part of this exciting moment. Twenty children might want to flock into the cushiony corner. Do you set up groups, for instance?

TRACY: We certainly do not provide badges to limit numbers in an area. It all comes back to the trust we have in the children, trusting that because they have framed that learning, they will use that area well. And that they will understand that if the area feels rather crushy or too tight, they need to think about moving on. Our children have learned that very quickly, because it is their environment and they want to look after it. We don't have to stop children clambering over each other and not respecting each other. That is because *respect* is modelled by the adults and portrayed by them.

FLEUR: You have seen settings where the respect is not there, and then there comes a need for greater control.

TRACY: Yes, but that is because the children do not have *ownership* of their space. Things they have not asked for through action or words clutter their space, and so they clamber over stuff to get what they want. They feel they must clamber over, because they have not been listened to. They may be saying by their clambering that they need more space. So what are we going to do about it? We are going to make more space, move more furniture. If more children want to use an area, we need to respond by enlarging the area, and making it more accessible.

FLEUR: So it's not a question of restricting the children, but increasing the area.

TRACY: Absolutely. The spaces evolve, areas become smaller or bigger as need be.

FLEUR: Do you think you need a very creative, flexible and imaginative person to work this way?

TRACY: I believe everybody has the capacity. And it is to do with that key word, 'reflection'. We all have the ability to be *reflective*; it all depends on whether we choose to use that skill. And it is through reflection, whether as a team or as children, that we can evaluate what is working or not working.

FLEUR: And because you work as a team, no one person need feel she is floundering; she can always take her thoughts to someone else to reflect on.

TRACY: Absolutely. We are all here to help each other. There is no hierarchy. Everyone is equal. The child's view is equally important. That is the main thing, because the children can then trust in the adults and trust in what we are doing with the environment, even when they are not here. They can trust that their creative work is still here in the morning, ready for them to take it forward.

FLEUR: So we have come round, right where we started. The children can trust that their things are in safe keeping.

Clearly, this trust hasn't happened overnight. Perhaps you can finish by describing your journey to this point.

TRACY: Yes, a long, long journey, but well worth it! It's about taking people with you; it's about developing and sharing the vision. Each of us is somewhere on our own learning curve. My vision – gained from working closely alongside children and observing them learning – is strong about how children should learn to their maximum capacity. It's through that vision that learning becomes powerful, but it does take a long, long time. It's a gradual, slow process.

FLEUR: I know that some of your staff came in over their holiday to reorganise a space. I know that you use veils, cloths and curtains to create an area – something suggestive and not too concrete, ephemeral and yet real.

TRACY: Absolutely. It provides flexibility. That adults come in to school in their own time shows their enthusiasm, their dedication, and their passion for working with children in this way. They can see the impact it is having on children and they are feeling it too, and learning is powerful when adults can learn alongside children, and this is where we are at the moment on our learning journey. And we will carry it on, and because you never do arrive, it will carry on for ever!

FLEUR: Thank goodness for that!

Reflections on visiting Tracy's school

I have made two visits to Tracy's school, one while the children were there and the other at the end of the day, to record the above conversation. The more I think about what I saw, the more I detect radical differences between her learning environment and the traditional nurseries with which I am familiar. In both, at first and superficial sight, children can be seen playing freely in areas of their choosing. A closer look reveals that Tracy's areas are envisioned differently. Gone are the set spaces called, 'The writing area' or 'Painting area' which define what you may do there. Instead, spaces have evolved in response to the interests of the children and the resources are available to allow them to use materials that suit their imaginative pursuits. There are pathways to reach needful resources and the whole space seems light, airy and clear of clutter. There is central space that allows the possibility of new directions to the children's play, which they can try out. New materials are introduced to provoke new avenues of enquiry. Furniture is not set and partitions are not rigid; areas are demarked by suggestive curtains, drapes and veils which give intimacy and imaginative scope. The use of mirrors and lighting adds further effects.

The areas grow as the children develop them. All areas are open to the central space which allows for new ideas to emerge; the enabling adults can easily observe, support and extend learning opportunities as they are invited into the play. The way is open to the outside and children can bring what they want from the outside to help in their enquiries and constructions.

There are no displays on the walls that are 'pretty' versions of children's products, framed by the adults' artistic notions. Instead, the process of a learning journey is documented with photos and quotations, and is available for the children, their parents and staff, working as a team, to consult and reflect on, determining together possible ways forward. It is work in progress, not a celebration of an end product. There are myriad possibilities and the way to proceed is open-ended. Because there is no knowing what fantastic ideas may emerge from the creative energy of the children, bouncing ideas off each other, there is no certainty about how a project might develop. I could see ideas from Reggio – but transformed to fit the conditions and culture of this school in Hartlepool.

Coming as I did from my 1960s perspective of child-centred learning, I was surprised to see a teacher-led session on phonics with an array of structured activities following on for groups of children. I was surprised how enthusiastically the children demonstrated for me the sounds that the letters could make and how eagerly they practised their phonics in their groups. Then came child-initiated time, and the children knew exactly where to go to continue with their creations, dramatic and constructive, from yesterday, using all the space available, indoors and out. This was not a random rush to do whatever caught their fancy, but an assured and purposeful return to work-in-progress, as agreed in reflective time. Too often, teacher-led activities with the whole class on the carpet are followed by an explosion into choosing, without any connections to the 'led' session or extensions of that learning into the free-play environment. This thought led me to consider the unfortunate fate of the idea of 'child-centredness' over the course of my career.

Reflections on child-centredness

My career spans from the Plowden Report in the 1960s to the newly instituted Early Years Framework in September 2009. In between, it has seen the National Curriculum, the Literacy and Numeracy Strategies, *Every Child Matters*, *Every Child a Talker*. I have maintained throughout the importance of being child centred, of listening to the child's interests and motivations, the belief in harnessing the natural curiosity and explorative urge of young children in the interests of their learning. I am happy to speak of the 'whole child' and the paramount importance of well-being and the wonder associated with discovery and achievement.

But because the role of the adult as partner and co-constructor of meaning was misunderstood, the notion of 'child-centredness' fell into disrepute. It was confused with a laissez-faire attitude of adults, leaving children to their own devices. Children were left to be creative in a sea of stimuli. A belief in innate creativity, an unfolding of talent – as a seed becomes a tree – meant that adult intervention was often seen as disruptive and repressive. Rousseau's Emile was largely a solo learner or pupil, maturing naturally, without interference.

Sweetness and light, however, did not guarantee learning in a bustling, pushing crowd. Everyone pursuing his own ends in a communal space could easily result in mayhem, a fighting for resource and space. There has always been a fear of anarchy and a need for conformity and standardisation. Often inspiration has been seen as dangerous and quirky rather than as necessary to new thought and innovation. So there is a backlash against too much freedom.

So to give shape and direction to activities, there comes the prescriptive curriculum to ensure that accepted standards are met. Unfortunately, the transmission of knowledge then becomes the focus and children increasingly become the passive recipients of an adult agenda. To counteract this tendency, teachers are exhorted to inject enthusiasm and creativity into the process. For me, however, there is a world of difference between an ideology that says, 'Play is a child's way of exploring and making sense', and one that says, 'Make your learning goals playful. Liven up your lesson plan with some playful elements and deliver it with enthusiasm.'

Creativity then becomes a strand to be woven in alongside numeracy, literacy, knowledge of the world etc. …

My feeling is that we keep throwing out the baby with the bathwater, as one ideology replaces another. Over my working life, there has been a pendulum at work here – a swing back, to balance too big a swing forward. We have traded in false dichotomies: structure versus freedom, work versus play; child-initiated versus child-led.

I feel that Tracy with her 'blended learning' keeps a desirable balance. She has created a democratic culture based on mutual respect, where the child's voice is listened to but where the enabling adult is ever vigilant. She has promoted the making of enriched environments, in which competent children and responsive adults can engage in thinking creatively together.

Rose reflects on areas in her nursery class

I had been thinking about the construction kits. They are enormously popular with a group of children. Certain children always start their day here, before gravitating elsewhere. We tend to think of this area as being about designing and making and developing physical skills rather than creativity. However, this may be our own construct of what is happening.

Take Paul, who plays here every day. Although he has other interests too – sand and the outdoor play environment in particular. He also constructs in the scrap materials area. He works mainly in 3D. When he works in 2D he becomes frustrated when he isn't able to represent the ideas he visualises.

He is brimming with creative ideas. He can build a super-hero vehicle with Mobilo and then transform it into a dog. Then one of his friends will make a dog and they play together with their models. For several weeks dogs had been a recurring play theme for Paul. He played dogs in the home corner and made a dog with scrap materials and a toy for his pet dog. At other times his constructions reflect the stories we have been reading. For a few days woodpeckers appeared made from magnetic prism shapes inspired by Goodnight Owl *(Hutchins, 1975). The next day he made a fox after we had been reading* The Treasure Hunt *(Butterworth, 1997). It is important to Paul to tell adults about his creations, what they are and what they can do. He explains everything in lots of detail. I wondered if he planned what he was going to make or whether his models emerged as he began to connect pieces together.*

For a week I focused on the construction kits so as to engage with the children and observe the creative process. So many models were being produced, so I began making a list on a big sheet of paper, writing down the names children gave their models. The children engaged with this idea. The models were far broader in scope than I had expected. There were some models related to super-hero TV programmes. Some of the vocabulary connected with these was unfamiliar to me, such as the 'transformer robot in the sky', but the children knew the language well and endeavoured to explain to me. There were lots of other vehicles and several animals, which led to groups of children engaging in imaginative play. One afternoon, several children made dinosaurs and then played under a table with their models. Often there was a link with play elsewhere, e.g. at this time dinosaurs were also popular in the sand, as were fiction and non-fiction books about dinosaurs. Often a model made with Mobilo was followed up with a model in the box modelling area. Several themes were flowing back and forth. Sometimes this was a theme followed by one particular child, but at other times a group would be engaged in a similar theme.

Transforming models was another aspect where it became clear that creativity was central. The idea of transformation may stem from TV programmes and associated toys, but it appeared a powerful idea to children to be able to transform a model into something else. There was an imaginative, open-mindedness in this process. The Mobilo construction kit is particularly well adapted for transformation, due to its flexible connecting components.

Children often work independently in this area, only calling on adults to help them when they struggle to connect the pieces or need help to find a particular part. Until now, when I have focused on this area it has usually been to encourage children to plan their models or use the instruction cards that come with the kits. I realise now that I was often missing the point, because actually the construction kits also provide a dynamic for creativity. It became clear the question about whether children knew what they were going to build was the wrong one. What I found when I engaged in a dialogue with the children was that they wanted to talk about what they had created, not about what they had planned.

If we can draw anything from this, it is that we need to approach the standard activity areas and resources in our early years settings with openness to their potential beyond the most obvious. When we watch and listen intently we will observe themes flowing in and out of different areas of the nursery. When we are alert to this we will see how those themes re-emerge in different areas or return a few days later. In our practice we need to be able to move with children to be part of this process, and we also need to ensure that daily dialogue takes place within our teams so that we share the themes and connect with them wherever they present themselves.

Take a tip

See whether you can unclutter your environment. Ask whether there are too many things that the children have not asked for, rarely make use of or regularly misuse. Is there unnecessary furniture? Are there clear pathways to allow children to access what they need? Is there space for new ideas to germinate?

Reading and resources

Duffy, B. (1998) *Supporting Creativity and Imagination in the Early Years*, Buckingham: Open University Press.

Robson, S. and Smedley, S. (eds) (1996) *Education in Early Childhood: first things first*, London: David Fulton Roehampton Institute.

Thornton, L. and Brunton, P. (2005) *Understanding the Reggio Approach*, London: David Fulton.

Story making

We owe much to Vivien Paley, kindergarten teacher, who wrote the stories of her classroom and reflected on her own role. She came to value the children's dramatic play, their rites and images, as the main incentive of the creative process. She saw newcomers to the classroom drift and worry until they were given a part to play. They gained a purpose and a place in the dramatic structure. The underlying themes of friendship lost and found are played out over and over again. Storytellers need listeners, so stories are not private affairs but a social phenomenon. The collective imagination colours classroom activities, binding children together. As she says:

> storytelling is contagious and listening to the children's stories will rekindle the teacher's. Once we push deeply into the collective imagination, it is easier to establish connections and build mythologies. The classroom that does not create its own legends has not travelled beneath the surface to where the living takes place. The fantasies of any group form the basis of its culture; this is where we search for common ground. That which we have forgotten how to do, children do best of all: they make up stories. Theirs may be the original model for the active, unrestricted examination of an idea.
>
> (Paley 1991: 5)

Reading and resources

Paley, V. (1991) *The Boy Who Would Be A Helicopter*, Cambridge, MA and London: Harvard University Press.

4 Creative conversations

The Talking Table

Fleur Griffiths

Fred talked to himself, rocking in his seat and not responding to the play of others around him. Listening in, I could catch the key word: 'transformer'; these mechanical toys and their language were being echoed with exact intonation. Sitting beside him with Playdoh, I transformed my dough from a ball into a sausage into a biscuit and commented on these transformations. Attracted by the word 'transform', he started to shape and reshape his piece, getting me to look. His mother and I talked about the need to attach language to the actions of the moment, and transforming Plasticene became a game at home. A lump of the stuff became his pocketed treasure to show at the Table. He demonstrated the transformations he could make, using appropriate language and communicating his message with proper eye contact. Nursery staff noticed that he was approaching adults with more smiles and was engaged with another 'friend' in games of the chasing variety, calling the child by name to join him.

From my A–Z of children who have visited me at The Talking Table, I have chosen Fred to help explain what the Table is and what makes it distinctive. The Table was devised in response to a request to help improve speaking and listening in nurseries in the north-east of England. Nursery staff were concerned that many children were making little imaginative use of the array of play possibilities on offer and adults were spending precious time settling conflicts or rearranging the setting, rather than interacting with children playfully. The Talking Table was to give them a more imaginative role. Fred's story underlines the need for a sensitive approach in the first place: I sit beside him, listen and watch, and then join in parallel play which echoes his preoccupation. This excites his interest enough to take notice and exchange glances. We begin to 'converse' around a topic of mutual concern, taking turns without speaking. This mirrors the 'dance' pattern of early mother-and-child communication, which is a collaborative and interactive experience from the start.

Because of my professional training, I can pick up quickly on someone like Fred, who is struggling to communicate with others. I am aware that silence is a communication, and I listen to the messages that body language and gesture bring. Rather than spend time diagnosing and labelling him, I seek to reach him through his *interests*, and slowly draw him into the social scene and *include* him in a circle of friends round a small table with four places. Circle Time techniques ensure that he will have a turn and be listened to with respect. The Table welcomes all comers and is not reserved for those with difficulties; we are in the mainstream and embrace the whole class. This is social inclusion in practice.

Most importantly, Fred's story shows that no child is seen as lacking in imagination – even children on the autistic spectrum, defined medically by deficits in imagination and social play. Fred could start to 'transform' one thing into another with his dough and thereby begin to exercise the imagination. He was no longer stuck in repetitive, static patterns of behaviour. He was not confined to spoken language to be understood, but could use another language from the many available to children, e.g. drawing and drama, gesture and facial expression. Round the Table, using our imagination, we are able to create stories from the disparate objects children bring. We create a dialogue around the different materials and use string or felt pens to make lines, enclosures, ladders, pathways which join our concerns together. We create contexts like the seaside or the park from marks of blue or green, and so-called scribbles become danger, jelly, mud or anything else we fancy. We can use our hands to knock on imaginary doors, to jump on trampolines, climb beanstalks, whiz down slides without leaving our seats. We can pick up play-people, teddy, power-ranger, toy animals as the character who converses with drawings, materials and involves the other children round the Table as a listening audience. Many children who would be silenced by direct questioning happily talk with a puppet.

Such playfulness is the stuff of creativity and comes naturally to children. Relaxed laughter releases energy to attend and learn. There is no pressure to answer in a particular way to adult questions. Instead, I follow the lead of the children and become a play partner. I have no agenda or lesson to deliver. I only seek to watch and join with the themes/schemas of the children.

Having made rapport with the nursery children on my first visit by playing alongside and being drawn in to their fantasies and concerns, I am ready to be visited at my special Table – a round table with chairs for four and covered with paper to allow a graphic language of communication, if need be. I am available in the nursery as a choice alongside painting, house corner, construction or Playdoh. I wear a blue tunic with coloured pockets from which peep enticing objects. The children too can bring their pocket-sized treasures to pass round and so reciprocate. In one pocket, I have a blue visitors' book in which I can enter the names of the children as they sit down. If a child is too shy even to give his name, others inform my waiting pen. This gives each child a sense of importance within the group. It makes for a sense of belonging to a circle of friends. Exchanging names is the basis for any communication and allows me to introduce and explain myself as well. For children to converse comfortably, it is useful for them to attract attention by using names. The writing of names establishes an orderly routine, a leisurely pace and a focus on each in turn. The record is also useful, as it shows up frequent visitors and the occasional child who might need a gentle introduction to participate.

My favourite companion is a beanie bear who invites curious questions about his name, his bandaged paw or party hat. As the children handle him in turn around the circle, they can decide to make him jump, dance, wave, clap hands, curl up or go to sleep. He is expressive enough to look sad, tired and happy and to reflect the children's moods. Some children say what they are doing, given a lead like 'I can make Teddy. … '; for the silent actors I can do a simple commentary. At the end of such a round, I can use him like a puppet to create the story of his journey. The children will answer for him or nod to approve my version of their involvement. I introduce the story with the age-old opening, 'Once upon a time … '. We may leave it here, or I may offer each child in turn a choice of colour from my pack of felt tips. From the marks made, another story can unfold. Thus we create stories around a shared experience. We construct meaning together. We make human sense together.

To mark the end, we roll up the communal paper, and this scroll is a book the children feel they own. They can interpret the marks on this communal paper from the Table and, with their objects as prompts, they can retell the story to others in the nursery and to their parents.

The direct involvement of parents is another vital ingredient of the Talking Table, as can be seen by the discussion with Fred's mother. A welcoming invitation goes out to all parents, explaining that Mrs G. (my persona) will be visiting every Wednesday for six weeks to encourage speaking, listening and storytelling. She will be found at a special round Table and wearing a blue tunic with colourful pockets full of objects to entice curious children to approach – and often to ask questions. So as to create the turn-taking pattern of conversation, the children can reciprocate by choosing something small and secret that they would like to show at the Table. Parents are invited to return to nursery half an hour earlier than pick-up, time to hear and see what the children have been doing. They can sometimes see video or photographs, and hear the stories told from the large paper. They can then have discussions around a Talking Table of their own. Comments collected from parents at the end of a conversation show that there have been changes in their relationships with their children, and to the learning contexts they have created in the home. They pick up on the idea of saying, 'I wonder whether ... ' when shown their child's artwork, instead of the difficult question, 'What is it?'

Parents' comments

- It's nice to hear what our children have been doing and saying. It is so difficult to get any idea from asking them what they did at nursery.
- I normally get no answer about school but when I said, 'I wonder whether ... ', he looked at me with a big smile and we got talking. I think he was surprised that I was playing rather than being anxious about it.
- When I did the 'I wonder' idea it turned into a guessing game. He kept saying, 'Guess again!'
- Before I finished saying 'I wonder', she told me in great detail what was going on in her picture. When her Dad said, 'What is it?' she shrugged and cast the paper aside. It's amazing what a difference it makes – how you ask a question.
- What I like is that the children are not pushed to come to the Table. They choose. The quiet ones like mine can watch and be part of the story too.
- I now try to look at things more from the child's point of view. I can see there is more in a line or mark on the page than I thought before.
- I am watching and listening better and being more like a partner when we do things.
- Whereas I would have said, 'Here's some paper and colour. Draw Mummy a picture', and then left her to do it while I did something else, I now sit down and join in more – with her permission, of course.
- Joining in with drawing has made stories much more imaginative. It used to be the same rainbow or the usual house with windows, doors, chimney and smoke and it never developed ... Now it can be very dramatic!
- When a picture came from nursery, I used to say, 'Lovely!' and stick it on the fridge. I now know there is much more to it and it can turn into a conversation.

The word conversation often has the word 'idle' in front of it. Much adult conversation is a form of politeness to pass the time of day. Most such approaches from adults to children are comments on their dress, hair, shoes, because they are immediately on view and bring a joint focus. Having something striking about your dress, tunic, hat, turns the tables and allows children to take the initiative and ask questions about you. My objects are personal and lead to curious questions. Teddy sticking out of my pocket attracts attention, and a bandage around his paw, a party hat or an umbrella invite enquiries. So the talk becomes two-way. The questions are not in one direction. The clues suggest possible story plots. In a social circle, stories are becoming shared and retold.

We are aiming for that *shared, sustained, thinking* – children wondering, speculating, coming to agreement or arguing. The whole conversation is thus lifted to a higher plane.

Rachael was full of ideas and always had a trail of children catching on to her dramatic train of thought in the home and dressing-up corner. She could also translate ideas into drawing and craftwork. Unless someone was alert to these stories, they were likely to evaporate into thin air. So it was good that she showed me her drawing at the Table, a page of colourful and energetic marks. First, we had a two-way conversation about fireworks, and soon she was able to tell the story all on her own to a listening audience. Holding Teddy as an actor, she told this story with the actions. 'Teddy was lying down looking at fireworks. He did not like the loud bangs of the rockets. He closed his ears with his paws. He liked the shooting stars and all the sparks high in the sky.' This time when she took her picture home, it was not passed over with a vague compliment, 'Nice dear'. Instead, Rachael came out with a full story of its meaning, without having to answer the deadening question, 'What is it?'

Not only are there conversations with parents, there is lunchtime talking with the staff involved. We become co-workers and reflective practitioners, carrying out the Plan, Do, Review cycle of Action Research. We make adjustments to the context, altering the place, the timings. At the outset, staff are given handouts about 'Conversational Principles' (Webster 1987: 27–31) and the 'Role of the Adult' (Duffy 1998: 140–41 cited in Griffiths 2002: 17–20), but it is expected that more can be learned from modelling than by instruction. Teachers can join the Table as participants, but I discourage the outsider, watching with clipboard. Some teachers are so in tune with the Talking Table and its child-centred approach that they feel able to do a Talking Table themselves very quickly. The following snow dialogue was given to me by Alison Martin, a teacher who saw me once and did her own sessions the next day. This conversation happened at the Table after a pretend snow-fall.

Snow dialogue

ABI: If you rub the lucky diamond a puppy comes. (*She rubs the diamond in the snow six times.*) I wish I had a tiger, ROAR!

ABI: Oh look, diamonds, I've got some skis, I've been skiing with just my jumper on. I was freezing like this, brrrrr.

ABI TO MADDISON: What's your name?
MADDISON: Belinda.
ABI: Do you want to come and ski?
MADDISON: Yes.
(*Both put fingers in the snow and together say*) 'Whee … round and round.
MADDISON: We are friends aren't we?
ABI: Yes.

Ali Martin

Teachers' views

- It takes us back to the child as the focus of attention rather than curriculum delivery. The child's agenda can be aired.
- It gives a way of getting to know the child and his/her abilities and interests.
- It is open ended; it can develop in many directions.
- It allows for joint working and is about sharing of ideas.
- Friendships can develop and children can feel they belong to the small group.
- It is great to have the time to give better listening attention.
- Children's vocabulary and imagination have developed.

- It depends on choice; children are not picked or pressured to do an activity.
- Their excitement and involvement can be seen on their faces.
- All children can take part and it has something for every level of ability. It is inclusive. It can be a secure place but yet offer challenge.
- It is based on storytelling and it can develop with everyone's contribution giving a push to the plot.
- It has increased staff confidence to try a new tool.
- It has an effect on behaviour because it recognises the need for approval and belonging. Certain attention-seeking children have calmed and sought to please.

Because there is link-up between all parties – school, home and visitor – and they are all communicating and conversing, querying and celebrating, the child's world makes more sense. *The child feels that there is always something to say to someone who cares to listen.* The adults are more tuned in to the interests of individual children and the children have a space to communicate these interests. They are not required to tell news, but to make up stories playfully together, a more congenial pursuit for children.

A further extension is passing what has been learned on to other settings. Schools have run workshops at conferences to illuminate what they see as the benefits and drawbacks of the Talking Table. In the next sections there follow some frequently asked questions from forums such as these, and my responses to these enquiries.

What happens once the special visitor leaves?

Part of the evaluation with staff at the end of an intervention is to consider the benefits and drawbacks of the Talking Table and to imagine how it might continue once the special visitor leaves. No one imagines that one member of staff can spend a whole session at the Table, talking and listening with children, however desirable that might be. It is possible, however, for an adult to put on a cloak or hat to signal availability for such a session. Once that adult is in role, she can only pay full attention to the children if she is freed from responsibility for housekeeping or supervising roles.

Most schools rotate staff to allow special activities to take place. Every child gets a chance to make that Mothers' Day or Easter card with an adult in attendance. If such can be done for this purpose, speaking and listening can be given the same priority in terms of staffing.

Many settings keep a day a week for Talking Table and maintain the habit of the children bringing a pocket-sized treasure from home. They manage this by having an opportunity for children to share their things on arrival, when excitement is at its height; the objects can then be kept safely in a mystery bag for use later.

Some schools use a Talking Table format as a review strategy towards the end of nursery. Models, drawings, stories or craft work can be the basis of a conversation celebrating these creations.

Talking Table has been kept on because of its celebratory and inclusive ways of involving parents. Letters home have suggested themes like bring something from the park or beach; the baker's shop; something blue or soft ... . Parents then take a group themselves. Older children in some cases have quickly learned how to do circle-time rounds.

How do you involve very shy children?

There are a range of reasons why a child may present as shy or silent, so there is no pat answer. Pressure to talk under a barrage of questions can make any one of us clam up. Fear of saying the wrong thing can also end up in silence. This underlines the importance of playfulness, which admits lots of answers and makes for relaxed laughter. Some children will sing along with others or join in a chant like 'Abracadabra'. Others will find a voice when manipulating a puppet or pretending to be someone else. It is easier to whisper to Teddy or show him around your space than to answer the teacher's questions, however sensitive.

The Talking Table respects a child's choice to remain silent, but to participate by listening and by doing something in turn. In early rounds, the adult puts the words to the actions and to the facial expressions she picks up. Often a nod or shake of the head will signal that you are on the right track. No child is dependent on speech alone to express herself; she is supported by the active context and the message is conveyed by gestures, pen marks and body language. Children inhibited by a speech defect or unused to English as a first language are saved from painful silences and requests to repeat themselves. Better for you to make a mistake of interpretation and misunderstand than for a child to feel a failure.

Because of this safety, those children whom staff expect to stay away are the very ones who attach themselves most closely to the welcoming adult who is always in the place where she can be found.

Beth had rarely been heard to speak in nursery and she tended to freeze and glaze over if addressed. She was reluctant to tell about the pictures she drew, which clearly depicted a scene from her experience of watching gulls at the seaside. Adding a person or a puppet to ask if he might join in got a quick nod. She liked to set out a scene from her Pooh Bear book and arrange play people around a handkerchief as the picnic cloth. The bear from my pocket could jump down to join the group. Others drew or provided food for the picnic. On one occasion, someone had an accident at the picnic and Beth came to the rescue, using the nurse puppet. The next week, Beth hovered around the Table, fingering the treasured object hidden in her pocket, but it was only at the end of the session that she burst out with the whole story without any help, standing up tall and stretching out the bandage she had brought:
'There is a story behind this bandage. Once upon a time, my granddad went to work and he cut his finger ... and it was bleeding ... and Nurse Beth came and made it all better.'
Mother, who had got no response to her questions about nursery, found the indirect approach brought a flood of response:
'I tried the "I wonder" idea, and it worked. Her grandmother asked Beth what she had done at nursery.' No reply. Then I said, 'I wonder whether you played in the sand', and straight away she came out with a whole string of things she had done.

Carol moved her chair up alongside and wanted me to draw for her and read to her. Any pressure produced a whining 'I can't', and a babyish voice. Separating from her mother had been painful, and my presence drew the lost and wandering child like a magnet to my side. How was I to empower her to use her voice and hands? We drew round her hands and children put little things in her palm. They happily talked about their treasures, lent to Carol like a gift. They were happy to symbolise their objects by outline or colour or model, or to mark their function with expressive lines and rhythms with a pen on paper. I could write the story using the 'Once upon a time' opening and check I had got it right. Over the weeks, Carol went from holding the felt tip with me to guide it, to creating her own marks and then telling staff and children her special story of the little fish who escaped the dangerous shark and played safely behind the weeds.

Das liked the silver box in my pocket. In turn, the children opened the box to reveal themselves in the mirrored lid or to twirl the crystal ball of rainbow colours. Some children make faces in the mirror and this can spark off talk about moods and feelings, likes and dislikes. Others respond to my lead of 'I wish, I wish ... '. Das, whose first language was not English, always took part in the action and one day came out with, 'I wish, I wish for a fish in a dish', much to everyone's surprise and delight in the rhyme. It prompted the singing of the local song, 'you shall have a fishy, in a little dishy, when the boat comes in'. He found comfort in the repetitive script and song, and in the wait-time listening to others to collect his courage.

How do you end a session?

The Talking Table is not a lesson that has to be completed. The teacher's agenda is not followed. The teacher is alert and open to what the children bring and invent. She facilitates the turn-taking pattern and gives each the chance to be heard in a round. Once round a circle has an obvious conclusion. The teacher uses the 'Once upon a time' to round off a joint story-making session. She can then thank each child in turn for helping the story along and say 'Goodbye and thank you for visiting'. Shaking hands to greet and farewell is liked by children as a mark of respect to each one. The teacher can then signal the end of that round by getting up and closing down the activity, drawing the chairs into the table. If the story has a shared piece of mark making, the paper can be ceremonially rolled up, with the children helping. The rolled-up story can then be put up elsewhere, and the children will gather round it and retell the story, especially if they have the character, like Teddy, as the pivot of the tale. Sometimes the paper is in the foyer, where parents gather, and the children tell their story once again to their parents.

In any group, there are those with very short attention spans and those who want to do artistic masterpieces slowly. Accommodating these extremes is difficult. So, early rounds need to be short: a simple pass of an object around the circle. This allows a quick changeover to include everyone in turn. You can promise a future return to someone who will not be moved! If artistic creation is something a child wishes to do and needs more time for, it helps the flow if this child is directed to the art area in the nursery to pursue her ideas, with a promise of a visit to her later. Those addicted to the Table will need to be prompted to choose another activity and come back when others have had a turn. That's only fair!

Adam loves to colour in, keeping within the lines with great concentration. He is the first to come and be welcomed and have his name entered ceremoniously in my blue visitors' book. Rather than speak, he settles to work on the communal circle of paper covering the surface of our round table, intent on making me a present of his drawing. I sense a tension in his fingers and face and an anxiety to please by being neat. His careful bands of colour seem not to represent something of personal importance and my 'Once upon a time … ' prompt draws a blank. Then, one morning, he goes from his perfect stripes of colour to a wild scribble of excited lines, saying, 'The house has gone all to pieces', but that there is nothing to worry about because he can build another one. Now, we have the beginnings of a meaningful story to talk about. Having expressed himself successfully, he is now ready to leave the Talking Table and I am able to say 'Goodbye, Adam, and thank you for visiting', as I do to each child. Greetings and farewells by name and even a little shake of the hand focus personal attention, and give prestige to comings and goings.

Do you have to have a table? Can't you just encourage interaction in the various areas?

Having the Table has given speaking and listening a higher profile. It has given staff a chance to practise conversational principles and become better listeners. They then become better play partners in other areas. It allows them to be more playful and flexible, and to worry less about delivering the curriculum. They find that the children are learning their colours, sizes etc. incidentally and remembering what they have learned in this playful manner.

Talking Tables occur wherever two or three gather round a shared interest. A ring of cushions on the floor can signal a discussion in the large construction area. Roll out a mat, or group around a hoop, and you have a natural circle to engage in creative conversation. One school has a Talking Tent outside.

The Talking Tent

A colleague of mine attended a Talking Table conference and returned to school feeling very inspired. We decided to find opportunities within the very busy day to have our own Talking Table. At the time we were looking at different ways to incorporate the outdoor learning environment into our day. We came up with the idea of using a tent outdoors and making this our 'Talking Table'. We use the tent in the same way you would use the table: children are free to come and visit and we also encourage the children to bring items of personal interest to share with us and Coogie Cat. We fill the tent with cushions, items of interest, blankets and, of course, the class soft toy, Coogie Cat, comes too! To start with, we placed cushions just outside the door of the tent so that children who might be slightly unsure of entering it could observe what was going on from a distance – now all of the children are very confident to visit!

We have found many benefits since the implementation of the Talking Tent: primarily, we have noticed that children who would tend to shy away from 'talking/speaking' activities are regular, confident visitors to the tent.

Although the Talking Tent is extremely popular in the outdoor environment, we have found that 'talking tables' can occur in many areas: for example, we have set out five cushions around a large mirror and have found that this works just as well.

Here are some comments from the children.

- We go inside of the tent and we all get a cushion. It is cosy!
- I like going inside the tent, we can go on a journey anywhere, and we can make a big map of what we can see.
- I like to visit Coogie Cat in the tent; we can bring things to tell him about.

We have found the notion of the Talking Table to be a fantastic way to encourage focused speaking and listening, mark making, turn taking and to develop storytelling skills – a quality time for all.

Kate Harbottle

Quentin came to nursery in a wheelchair. He badly wanted to join in with the children at play but it was happening all too fast around him. Having a still place at the Talking Table and an assured turn to handle the toys and participate made a huge difference to him. He loved to sit Teddy on a little cushion and explain to him. He rescued him when he got egg on his face and let him drink the orange he had drawn for him on his own section of the communal paper.

Polly was concerned that Teddy was covered in mud, and in answer to my general question, 'Oh dear! What shall we do?' she excitedly offered, 'I have an idea', and rushed off to the dressing-up corner. She returned in her favourite fairy costume with her magic wand to put things right and make him whole again. All the children in the group joined in the 'Abracadabra' spell and felt part of the solution.

Grace favoured the painting easel and freely made careful blobs of colour; she was clammed shut if asked about her paintings. They were probably pre-representational experiments in colour and brush-stroke. At the Talking Table, she listened in to others taking a line for a walk and visiting each other's worlds. She then announced her swirl to be a 'rosette' and nursery staff filled in with the news that she had won such a prize in a dancing competition. Grace was pleased to be the central character and this limelight led her on a path of self-expression. I thought how important it is to recognise the many languages of children and to give them the words to translate one language into another.

What objects do you find work best?

- **Personal treasures** work best because you enjoy them and others are given the privilege of handling them. Loans have more preciousness.
- **Favourite treasures** have included tickets, family photographs, jewels and make-up, masks and mirrors, Dinky cars and model animals, as well as grown-up items like torches or phones. Restricting the size of objects has prevented showing off with commercial toys, and instead has allowed children to find shells and stones and dead creatures to smuggle in to show. A dead spider hidden in a box has been a most productive stimulus! Other finds from pockets have been things to smell, to sound, to stroke – things that each child wishes to sense or activate in turn. Everyone wants to make the acrobat somersault down a ladder, and we can all chorus cautions like 'Be careful; Hold on tight; Concentrate; Don't fool about; Ready, Steady, Go!. … '. To take on the language of the controlling adult and reverse roles seems to incite both quiet ones and foolhardy ones to join in the game. You can see it is a game because there is so much laughter.
- For learning turn taking, **means-ends toys** work well: a button to press, something that winds up or spins, that makes music or sound, that tumbles down a ladder or jumps from a box. I have a woodpecker that pecks down a pole, and each child has a distinct turn.
- **Coloured pens** dictate content: black so often signals bad temper and danger; blue calls up water and sky; green becomes a beanstalk or garden; brown becomes mud or chocolate; red for blood; yellow for sunshine. …
- Children love **surprises** so boxes, pockets, bags and parcels intrigue. There is suspense while we guess what might be rattling inside. Hiding and seeking are important. Mystery bags are ever popular.
- Simple **enclosures** drawn on the paper can keep objects safe. Pieces of string, pipe cleaners and ribbon can demark areas: homes, gardens and parks.
- Other **objects bring power**: cars, planes, trains, keys, magic wands, webs, puppets, rings and jewels, money and magnets. These more symbolic objects make for more imaginative stories than the static possibilities of a power-ranger or Spiderman – although these figures are often the children's choice.
- **Things that can transform** also convey power: magnifying glasses, tools, masks, mirrors and even lumps of Plasticene or dough. Looking through a long tube or through coloured cellophane leads to 'I spy' turns. Shining a torch focuses attention.
- There are objects that prompt more altruistic control. Teddy is helped, washed, fed, rescued and told off! Reversal of roles is very satisfying – being the adult and caring for the **little baby or small animal** is the stuff of many stories.
- There are objects that touch on **adventure** and danger, mishap and fear. With them come the comforts and solutions, the rescues and havens. Plasters and bandages bring on a stream of disaster tales! Witches, giants and monsters can appear just from the use of a black crayon, a hole in the paper, a scribble.
- **Journeys** feature heavily in stories, so the planes, trains and cars can have another innings! It is easy to make trails, maps, roads and routes, stepping stones, ladders and bridges to create journeys. Tickets tell a tale. Natural objects like stones, pebbles, leaves, feathers, shells and pods can be found along the way.
- **Celebrations** need balloons, bubbles, party hats, jewels and presents, candles and cakes.

Jane had a birthday and brought a candle from her caterpillar cake. This prompted a flurry of birthday drawings: cakes and candles, balloons and party hats, food and presents. From my pockets came some presents, surprises in fancy boxes. There was singing of 'Happy Birthday', giving and opening of pretend presents and blowing out of pretend candles, and even popping of balloons by naughty Teddy.

What do you do about bad behaviour at the Table?

In the context of storytelling, there is no such thing as bad behaviour: angry holes in the paper, black scribbles and taking another's space can all be transformed by the imagination of the adult into the plot.

Eve carefully drew the classic house: four windows and a front door, and a chimney with smoke. Flowers grew in the garden and I added some of my own, with her permission. Suddenly she was upset by her neighbour, Frank, thoughtlessly crashing his Dinky car right into the flowers. What could we do? She would build a fence to keep him out but he kept coming up and banging into the fence. So what could we do? She put a small door in the fence and if he knocked, Frank could come in. She then could show him round and they could play in her bedroom with special toys. He could always ride away at speed, up hill, down dale, over and under bridges on the special track drawn with him on the next-door piece of paper.
I could model greetings and goodbyes and the language of negotiation so that the conflict could be resolved, using the children's solutions in a playful way.

Ken circled around the Table dressed as a tiger from the dressing-up corner. He tried to frighten with roars and claws. I asked the children if we could invite the tiger to tea, and luckily he was flattered into sitting with us and we all had a chance to try his tiger gloves. Each time thereafter, he came angrily making holes in the paper with a stabbing pen. His stories were of dungeons and disasters, but once his black mood was recognised and a given a narrative outlet he was less aggressive to children in play. He was learning the labels for his feelings so as to articulate them – an early step towards emotional literacy

Lesley, similarly, grabbed the black pen and made a hole in the paper with heavy strokes. The children gasped, expecting a telling-off, but were relieved when this potential upset became an enjoyable story for us all. By bringing Teddy to the scene of the black hole, I pretended he was afraid of what might be in the dark. Tentatively, Teddy stretches out his paw and pulls it back in mock horror. Lesley's story then becomes: Once upon a time Teddy put his paw down the black hole and the monster bit him. Others add bandages and comfort for poor Teddy. Lesley too is consoled, having entertained the circle and come from the position of outsider into the centre.

Ian scribbled in black with energy and resisted my guesses about smoke, spaghetti and water pools. Above the black, he drew a snake very carefully and made bands of colour to create his 'rainbow snake'. He always started with frantic circular scribbling and did offer that the black centre was 'a scary place' and the quieter border was 'a safe place'. His drawings reflected his changing mood and reflected a story of fear and sanctuary.

Establishing turn-taking rules at the outset helps prevent snatching, shouting, or butting in. Expecting a round to take place, however short, begins the process of respecting each person's contribution, a sharing of time and space. Early rounds simply share an interesting toy of the means-end type, something like a torch, a top, an opening box, a mystery bag. Each one has a clear turn before passing on. Respect for each in turn is established. When you move on to sharing a large piece of paper, much scribbling on top of someone else's contribution is prevented if we feel the space in front of us and claim as ours what we can cover with our two hands. Borders are where our fingers touch. Some children draw a safe area for themselves within which to draw.

Politeness is strongly modelled. Every child is welcomed, and thanked for coming. Goodbye and a handshake mark a departure. Permission is asked for entry to someone's space and Teddy will knock on an imaginary door to be shown around.

I have only once rescued bear from ill-treatment, and launched into a 'Once upon a time, poor bear ... '. Rescue stories are close to children's hearts and usually touch sympathies. They are full of ideas on how to make bear feel happy or what could entice the confiscate treasure to come out of hiding!

What do you think is important about this approach?

Reasons for the marked increase in language use and self-confidence noted by parents and teachers suggest themselves. Being able to express what is important to you and to feel listened to and appreciated brings gains in confidence and a sense of well-being. That leads to more approaches and more practice. The agenda is not mapped out in advance with cognitive targets in view, but the emotional import of the communication guides the process in a flexible way. Children are able to have conversations around things of mutual interest in an atmosphere of respect and relaxation. There is no right or wrong answer, so the pressure to satisfy some standard is removed. What makes human sense is what counts, and vocabulary comes in to help articulate meanings, which are often conveyed by body language and other expressive arts. It is an approach which hears the many languages of children.

Learning to read and write before you are adept at self-expression is to invite failure. Creating stories around drawings and models provides an important step towards appreciating storylines. Children can be agents and actors in the process of making stories. The adult joins these imaginative adventures, steering and stimulating new ideas, rather than *delivering* a language/literacy curriculum to passive subjects. Language learning requires a dialogue to take place in a specific context, and meaning can then be constructed together. Weak children are not targeted for help but the intervention is open to all in an inclusive spirit.

Yet while children have the chance to initiate and lead, the adult is actively engaged as a support and leader. Her role is to be like a more able friend who can empathise, but also challenge by introducing extensions to the learning. Children can feel secure in the turn-taking rules and the conventions of politeness modelled for them by the adult. S/he is in a predictable place and wears a familiar outfit and is free to listen. She can be relied on to contribute her own experience and provide enabling scripts. She is playful and yet making sure there is fair play.

She is neither an insider (a member of regular staff) nor an outsider (an observer or judge). She is a colleague and a parent/partner. She is not there to comment on shortcomings or to reveal deficits but to empower the participants. Parents can stop being surrogate teachers instilling knowledge and enjoy being play partners instead, using the 'motherese', which usually comes naturally. Parents come to enjoy hearing about the creativity of their children.

Watching a model, nursery staff feel that they can expand their role and give more prominence to the affective curriculum and to speaking and listening. They see how circle time fits in and how imaginative storytelling can be encouraged. It renews their belief in the education of the whole child and gives them courage to resist attempts to co-opt the nursery into a pre-school institution. They can go beyond simply getting children ready for school in a narrow sense: with colour and number concepts intact, and conforming behaviour. They can play to children's strengths: their sense of wonder, their playful imaginations and their need to belong.

Take a tip

Try the 'I wonder' idea, taken up so easily and successfully by parents. Most parents find that their requests for information about nursery are met with a shrug, a stare or a fob-off response from their children. Their questions do not trigger a communicative exchange of a sustained or meaningful nature. Simply by refraining from direct questioning and substituting a guess or a surmise works wonders in eliciting engaged conversation. The anxiety on both sides is lessened. Take away the pressure to answer a question, and talking and sharing happens.

Reading and resources

Duffy, B. (1998) 'Talking with and listening to young children', in S. Smidt (ed.), *The Early Years: a reader*, London: Routledge.

Edwards, C., Gandini, L. and Forman, G. (eds) (1998) *The Hundred Languages of Children: The Reggio Emilia approach – advanced reflections*, London: JAI Press.

Farmer, M. and Griffiths, F. (2006) 'The Talking Table: a case study', in J. Ginsborg and J. Clegg (eds) *Language and Social Disadvantage*, New York and London: Wiley, 165–76.

Griffiths, F. (2000) 'Play partners: parental involvement in a pre-school project for children with communication difficulties', in S. Wolfendale (ed.) *Special Needs in the Early Years: snapshots of practice*, London: Routledge.

——(2002) *Communication Counts: speech and language difficulties in the early years*, London: David Fulton Publishers.

Griffiths, F. (2008) *A–Z of Visitors to The Talking Table*, Gateshead: Gateshead Council Raising Achievement Service. Booklet produced for in-house teachers' conference, July.

Massey, S.L. (2004) 'Teacher–child conversation in the preschool classroom', *Early Childhood Education Journal*, 31 (4), 227–31.

Mosley, J. (1996) *Quality Circle Time in the Primary Classroom*, Cambridge: LDA.

Siraj-Blatchford, I. and Sylva, K. (2004) 'Researching pedagogy in English pre-schools', *British Educational Research Journal*, 30 (5), 713–30.

Tizard, B. and Hughes, M. (1984) *Young Children Learning: talking and thinking at home and at school*, London: Collins.

Webster, A. (1987) 'Enabling language acquisition: the developmental evidence', British Psychological Society, *Division of Educational and Child Psychology Newsletter*, 27, 25–31.

Wells, G. (1987) *The Meaning Makers; children learning language*, London: Hodder/Stoughton.

Wood, H. and Wood, D. (1988) 'Questioning the pre-school child', in A. Cohen and L. Cohen (eds), *Early Education; the pre-school years*, PCP.

Vygotsky, L.S. (1962) *Thought and Language*, Cambridge, MA: MIT Press.

5

From 'scribble' to story

Making sense of children's drawing

Fleur Griffiths in conversation with Marysia Holubecki

> How can we respond to early mark making? How can we show the same degree of interest that we show in realistic drawings? We can begin with a look at the actual 'doing' – the movements, the vocal sounds, the sheer sensuous pleasure of playfully handling sheets of paper and markers. And the utter surprise and delight in seeing what happens.
>
> (Kolbe 2003: 8)

This chapter is about such moments of shared delights around drawing. It highlights the role of the adult, who has the power to enhance or deflate a child's drawing intentions. If the adult sees children's drawings as developmental steps from artless scribbles to commendable representational skill and her role as facilitating this progress, then the dynamic power of these early marks is unrecognised. Alternatively, if the adult sees every attempt as 'self-expression', she will stand back so as not to inhibit the flow. The role favoured, however, is to be a conversational partner. To be avoided are uneven conversations where the more powerful one asks the questions and steers the novice towards more desirable outcomes. There are more equal exchanges: the adult is truly curious to know what the activity means for children and stands back to listen and watch, intervening to share the experience and to join in the meaning making.

The adult follows the lead the child gives. The lead is not necessarily verbal; the clues may lie in the pencil hold, the pressure or direction of the strokes, the frown of concentration, the sigh of contentment or the accompanying song. Just your presence and a smile of recognition about the mood of it may be enough. Sometimes the marks on the page represent the rhythms of a song, with a temporal, not a visual meaning. Sometimes the marks may have several or changing meanings, as a story unfolds. A well-meaning grown-up can halt the unfolding sense of it by the deadening question, 'What is it?' Silence can be the answer to an impossible question. The child comes to understand that the expectation is for him to represent the 3-D world – something he did not intend to do. He then draws to please the adult, not to represent his own thoughts and understandings. We get stereotypical houses or the child pesters us to draw something, not feeling up to the task himself.

As adults, we can recapture something of the fascination of making marks when we step in the snow, follow bicycle tracks in the dust, trace the pattern at the bottom of our pudding bowl or create bark or leaf rubbings. Children's marks on paper recreate such movement ideas. A swirl with paint is like water 'going down a plughole' (Athey 2003: 142). Children use the language of lines. Initially, children do not set out to depict an object in a representational manner, but more often a random explorative 'scribble' suggests to them a similarity; it looks like a 'ball' or a 'snail' or 'an airplane landing'. These are imaginative symbols and come straight from active experience. To make such associations seems to be deeply satisfying. With practice, the child can deliberately direct his lines to re-create those meanings.

So simple maps represent the common experience of walking a familiar route and mark the 'trajectory' from one point of interest to the next. Ponds and puddles are common content in such drawings and these are enactments with the pencil rather than visual copies. This is how drawing is understood at the Talking Table. I have reserved a frequently asked question to explain my use of drawing as communication.

How do you use drawing at the Talking Table?

I find that when I look imaginatively at so-called 'scribble', the marks yield up their meanings. I say playfully, 'It looks like spaghetti', or 'The knitting-wool has got all tangled up', or 'That looks like a scary place'; children reject or adopt a scenario that fits their mood or intentions. This way the seeds of a possible story are sown and the children can choose to water them.

The chosen colour also has meaning. A child may not know the names of colours but he has chosen a favourite for a personal reason. If a child chooses black and stabs at the paper with dagger-hold, with gritted teeth and deep frown, it is not difficult to read the message: 'Wow, that's an angry black!' I may say, and frequently this leads to a nod and a story starts to relieve the tension. Asking, 'Are you angry?' would most likely receive no response or an intensified scowl. Look at a dense black patch and a hole in the paper and ask whether it is safe to come near the edge; suddenly there are monsters or demons conjured from the depths. Watch a child dreamily slide the blue pen in wavy movements and tentatively guess: 'That looks like lazy blue-like waves?' Sometimes the answer comes without words: a boat shape appears and perhaps we can go for a ride. Real objects mingle with the lines and shapes: a jewel is safely enclosed in a drawn 'box'; the car is in a 'garage' and a horse is in a 'field'. Pass a real key and children pretend to open drawn doors to reveal their treasures. Something unexpected can happen: the jewel may be stolen, the horse escape or the car race to the seaside.

While the children draw, I leave them be and get on with making simple shapes of my own choosing: a round orange with my orange pen; stepping stones across a stream; stairs leading upwards, zigzags of danger ... These simple representations stand for a recent experience, a mood or a possible journey and are not representational art attempts. When it is my turn, I may say, 'I had an orange for breakfast; it was hard to peel but it tasted delicious', and I mime the happening at the same time and may even pass each child a pretend segment. So, the meaning is so much more than the mark alone can convey and it invites others to share in it. Meaning is conveyed as a personal story.

Writing down what the child says makes the bridge to literacy. It becomes clear that words have written forms, and children feel they are authors. They remember what they have said and soon can retell the story. I look at a faint, round shape, drawn with dots for eyes, and the inscription says, 'This is my Dad. He is having a cup of tea.' A wild splash of orange means 'the rabbit is running into the road – he gets squashed'. The story is so much more than the suggestive line or colour and can extend beyond the graphics. This is failure proof: no one can deny a personal meaning. To end up with a story that interests your friends round the Table makes you feel good. A creative conversation has taken place. The conversation peters out if a child simply serves up a routine picture that has no social dynamic, as can be seen in the following stories from the A–Z collection:

Mary deftly drew a round with two dots for eyes, a blob for a nose and a turned-up mouth, announcing: 'A smiley face'. She blankly insisted it was a face in response to my efforts to give the face a name, even her own name. The standard opening from me: 'Mary is smiling because ... ?' brought no flicker of invention. This was my first meeting with her and she was expecting praise for her perfect face, reproduced according to adult tutoring, and was puzzled by my playfulness. I remembered she had come to nursery with a toy rabbit so I answered my own question: 'I think Mary is smiling because she has her special rabbit with her today.' This brought a nod and a smile and soon her rabbit was drawn alongside. Instead of a sterile skill – that of drawing a face in a meaningless context – she welcomed a personal narrative which made sense of the activity.

Nelly, her opposite partner, responded with a sad face and she shook her head at every one of my reasons for her sadness. My guesses, however, interested her and she came up with her own story at the end. Here were two very able girls whose imagination was given little rein because they had been taught how to draw a face to meet the target for that achievement.

In conversation with Marysia

Marysia shares this concern about clever girls whose creativity could be curtailed and opportunities for their development missed:

> Girls are often quicker in their pencil control and their early artwork may be obvious and representational enough that it may seem to negate the need for a creative conversation to be held. This could be seen as a missed opportunity, the danger being, I feel, that creative development is, ironically, curtailed rather than encouraged.

She feels that boys are often disadvantaged too, because of not fulfilling adult expectations of neat representational drawing. The dynamic storytelling aspects are missed. She feels this happened in the case of her son Oliver.

The case of Oliver

Marysia sets the scene

Oliver, my son, is now 6 and his artwork is certainly now much more recognisable and possibly even more typical of his age and interests. He is more bothered now that it doesn't look right or isn't as 'good', neat and representational as others and it is with some sadness that I recognise his dilemma and wonder which kind of creativity will 'win'; the free, artistic, aesthetic story side or the graphic, representational skill side? He is still, however, keen to draw and paint and keeps hold of the stories behind the pictures.

And these stories are where we start, Oliver aged 2, four or so years ago, enjoying art using a variety of methods to make his stories visual and, I think, to communicate them to others. There is nothing exceptional in that, but what perhaps is critical is how the art is explored and encouraged, what questions and interest are shown, and when and by whom. What I am alluding to are the opportunities to encourage or discourage creativity and to use labelled praise, or indeed criticism, however well intentioned, with very young children's artwork. For example, a girl of similar age showing an interest in drawing and colouring-in may have received those first, arguably pivotal comments of 'how clever, how neat, how tidy'. These comments may well have been delivered with good intention quite naturally and understandably to a small child eager for praise and attention and approval. But does this translate into an understanding, on the child's part, that the 'tidy' art story, the less creative picture, is better somehow? That rows of identical flowers all coloured in beautifully that don't need elaboration are best? That progress will be commented on and judged by the developments and refinements of the appearance of a house with spiralling smoke out of the chimney, a small strip of grass, a small strip of sky and a smiling quarter-sun in the top left-hand corner.

The other side of coin is the child, much like Oliver, who isn't really scribbling but may well be perceived to be and who receives, again, well-intentioned comments that encourage him not to scribble but to be neat and tidy and to colour inside the lines! The message probably being that neatness, with recognisable, obvious content, is best and certainly desirable for a flying start at school.

Some of Oliver's early methods of communicating were by map making, often showing a journey, with events and characters along the way. (See map of Thoralby.)

Another was to use, literally as a vehicle for story, the farm machinery that so fascinated him from an early age. And the story would be about the rolling bales, smaller and smaller in the distance, and him being the tractor driver, not that this was a piece of representational landscape art, it wasn't a real image, but a concoction of his imagination creating a narrative.

The coloured plates (pages 8, 9, 10) are a very small selection of Oliver's pictures, all shrunk from about A3 size. Accompanying each is, in his words, a brief description of the action or the story. I had scribbled his thoughts at the time of painting on the backs of the pieces of artwork, but checked them out with him more recently. While his vocabulary has developed somewhat, the interpretations were all the same. He remembered very clearly doing each one and actually seemed really to enjoy having the opportunity to remember, relive and retell them with sound effects and dramatic gestures.

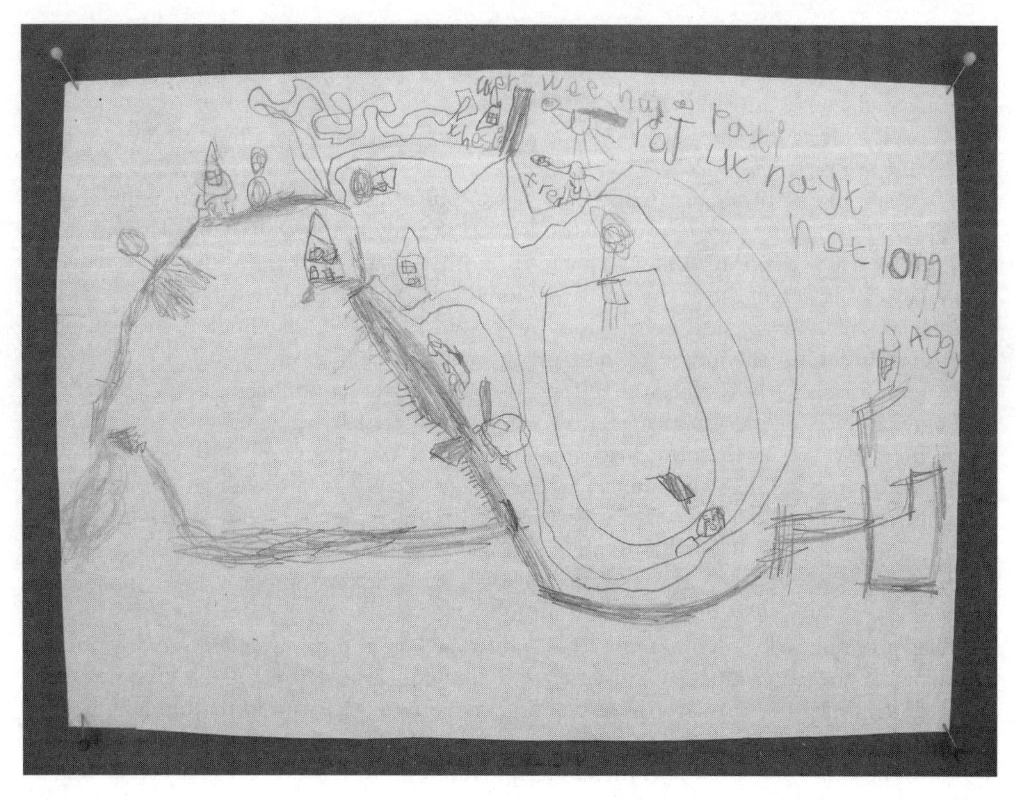

Map of Thoralby

Talking with Fleur about Oliver's pictures (see *Oliver's Paintings Tell a Story* in the plate section)

FLEUR: The first two paintings are beautiful patterns, aren't they?

MARYSIA: Yes, what first struck me about these pictures was that they were patterns: I could see symmetry, careful use of colour in an abstract design. I had no idea what they were.

FLEUR: Yet they were clearly representing something important for Oliver.

MARYSIA: Yes, it was only talking about it with him afterwards that I realised there was a story in his lines of colour.

FLEUR: And very complicated stories about the universe and the spiral arms of the galaxy, the phasers and the radar!

MARYSIA: They were about his early interest in space, which has developed over time, and is still with us today with rockets, planets and galaxies.

FLEUR: This suggests very factual, objective interest.

MARYSIA: Yes, he likes facts and he likes to gather facts and put them together. But he has emotional responses to the planets and he has personal relationships with them. He drew Pluto in the top corner of the page, banished as a planet from the 'Nooniverse'. Pluto was left out, which upset him – it was like losing your identity.

FLEUR: Yes I know his space-play is all about relationships, dangers, rescues with him in the driving seat winning out; friends and foes. It is difficult to represent all this in a picture – there is so much that is unspoken, so much more than meets the eye. So we are lucky that Oliver has the ability to explain, more than a year after the event.

MARYSIA: Yes, he really enjoyed looking at them again and having the chance to talk about them – like looking through a photograph album and reminiscing happily. Certainly his vocabulary and grammar were more developed than when he was 3, but essentially the meaning, the content of the pictures has remained constant. He had no need to change his story. He is not trying to elaborate to please me, but is faithful to his original intention, it seems. It shows that his stories even at a young age were elaborate enough – he did not need to add to his story later.

FLEUR: In our second pairing of pictures done when he was about three, there is a definite personal purpose in doing them: to give them to Aggie, his grandmother …

MARYSIA: …His grandmother, who has been his main carer while I worked, and for whom he has a deep love. He makes them as a gift in the knowledge that she will be pleased. There is a reciprocal arrangement in place. He will get much positive feedback because she is bound to be delighted. The more I look at these pictures, the more I realise they are not landscapes; he has plucked elements from his bank of experiences of the Safari park – a mixture of facts of interest and affection – and he has chosen to bring them together in one place in a narrative structure within the picture. For example, we see Aggie with her new walking stick, a symbol of her age and frailty and possible need of help and his protection … but things are well with the world, as can be seen by the huge sun and bright blue sky. Then there is the grand Sequoia tree, which fascinated him in a video. It is essentially a collection of favourite things, come together in an act of the imagination – in a story.

FLEUR: With a location and a main character who is so amazed by the Sequoia that her eyes are actually popping out of her head! … And what about the giraffe picture?

MARYSIA: Again, Oliver, who loves books and videos of animals, has chosen elements to make an imaginative landscape for a new story, all his own. They are not simply a list of objects but a narrative creation with a *relation* between the things. Again you have time of day – the shiny sun is going down to sleep, the giraffe is nibbling the grass – everything is in its rightful place – everything is cared for and doing what it needs to be doing.

FLEUR: And now we come to the final pairing of pictures we have chosen. These, I suppose, show what the effects of schooling or adult expectation might be. There are some signs of inhibition.

MARYSIA: I think it is more about him having to face certain restrictions imposed by a set task, which has a right and wrong way of doing it. It is this kind of dilemma that I was alluding to earlier. Oliver is still a child who wants to tell an imaginative story through art but the skill of being artistic presents an alternative choice to him. He also has to fulfil the demands of a school task: i.e. draw his visit to the cheese market.

FLEUR: His first impulse is to give the visit its emotional colouring: the black clouds, lashing rain, tent held down by heavy bricks, windscreen-wipers whirring … The elements affecting him and his friends.

MARYSIA: Yes, a very elemental thing. That day it was raining very heavily, and being out in it was very exhilarating and overwhelming. He turns that experience into *Star Wars* – something scary. He is reaching out to find the vocabulary to describe the powerfulness of the physical elements … and the cheese was secondary.

FLEUR: So, we see art slowly being affected by the expectations of the culture, and our concern is that children's need to express themselves imaginatively is not derailed by these imposed tasks.

MARYSIA: I think it is about working out what your aims and objectives are. Even though you have a curriculum to work to, there is still a lot you can do not to miss opportunities for children to be creative. We can be hung up on an adult agenda of learning objectives – like knowing the colours of the rainbow in the spectrum, or the prices of cheese for mathematical understanding. We are in danger of failing to realise that children learn in more creative ways if we are on the lookout.

I know that Oliver is a child who has had the benefit of a rich environment in terms of my interactions with him and other resources: who has been well supported with play opportunities and freedoms to explore and encouragement to make sense of things. And what I would say is that every child deserves those freedoms and those encouragements. And clearly many children are denied such opportunities. I work with children for whom this is the case.

FLEUR: I was going to ask you about your work on parenting programmes. It seems many of the strategies put over on those programmes have general application for all children.

MARYSIA: It is interesting that the programmes don't mention art as such, but are to do with emotional well-being, emotional resilience, good communication, positive relationships – the kind of thing that helps children be well-rounded and to communicate with the world in a positive way, and the principles behind these programmes accord with our idea of creating positive interactive opportunities. If we create good relationships around creative activity, we will be creating good relationships generally with our children.

Parenting programmes

The principles and suggestions of good practice in these programmes have a common-sense feel and can be carried out at home by any adult in an active relationship with a child. When art is used as a vehicle to understand meaning, as well as enhancing the creative potential of a child, the relationship is enhanced; improved emotional and social well-being of the child will give the child an inner resilience to call on.

In the **Mellow Parenting Programme** the following dimensions of parenting are used to identify and concentrate on the building blocks of positive relationships. Many aspects of these dimensions can be found in the simple activity of a child painting with an adult.

Anticipation: the adult prepares a child for the next step, using appropriate timing.

Responsiveness: the adult and child act in a reciprocal way and have fun together. There is both stimulation and affect. Examples would include approval, laughter and smiles, affectionate touch, gentle handling and care taking, all with appropriate body language in tune with what is being vocalised.

Positive autonomy: the adult shows an awareness of a child's individuality, wishes, needs and feelings and the need to exercise a choice.

Cooperation: child and adult are compliant with each other and able to negotiate.

Distress is dealt with positively by comforting, explaining, encouraging, enabling and using positive affect or tone and physical contact.

The Webster Stratton Incredible Years Programme places special emphasis on play and praise and building self confidence as fundamental building blocks of positive relationships.

Some guidelines

- Value and give full attention to your child's play (creative) activities.
- Listen to your children. Don't pressure the child to speak. Ask open questions: 'I wonder if … tell me about this. … '. Avoid over-questioning.
- Reinforce your child's efforts by describing what s/he is doing, with descriptive, labelled comments, e.g. 'I like the way you are using the brush like that, mixing those colours together'.
- Offer advice only when the child asks for it.
- Follow your child's lead (to include non-verbal communication).
- Spend regular time, when you have energy and emotional space to give.
- Try to resist giving too much help; encourage problem solving.
- Don't save praise for a perfect example.
- Give labelled and specific praise.
- Praise with smiles, eye contact and enthusiasm. Use pats and hugs and kisses.
- Give positive praise and praise immediately and consistently.
- Praise in front of others if there is an opportunity.
- Label the child's feelings and yours about accomplishments, e.g. 'You really seem happy with that … I am proud of you.'
- Laugh and have fun.

Take a tip

Become a watcher. Notice when children concentrate and are absorbed. Notice how they enjoy playing with colour, shape and form. Watch their hands and faces for clues to their intended meanings. Listen to what they say or sing, to sighs or whoops of delight. Give them time to explore and finish. Give them the best quality materials you can so that they can best form their drawing stories. Appreciate what they make – even a smile will serve. Let them tell you what their marks mean if they wish; beware of intrusive questioning.

Reading and resources

Athey, C. (2003) *Extending Thought in Young Children: a parent–teacher partnership*, London: Paul Chapman.

Kolbe, U. (2003) *It's Not a Bird Yet: the drama of drawing*, Byron Bay, Australia: Peppinot Press.

——(2007) *Rapunzel's Supermarket: all about young children and their art*, Byron Bay, Australia: Peppinot Press.

Mellow Parenting Programme, www.mellowparenting.org.

Webster-Stratton, C. (1990) *The Webster Stratton Incredible Years Programme*, Seattle, WA: Webster Stratton Program, www.incredibleyears.com.

Story telling and story acting

Putting positive interaction into action

Evi Typadi and Karen Hayon

I feel different when I interact with the children now. The children know I'm going to wait and they come and talk more.

The children stay longer interacting with me, so I am able to follow their interest and feed in the right words. I was waiting for a little girl to initiate and because of my waiting, she drew her family and then I commented. She repeated the words and said something else. Usually I would have asked her questions and she wouldn't have said anything.

Practitioners talking

How can we encourage children to speak more, and more creatively, in early years settings, so that they can practise this new skill that has been acquired relatively recently in their short lives? How can we help children to make connections with and learn from each other? How can we support the language development of all children? How can we help early years practitioners to identify and support children with language and communication difficulties?

These are the fundamental issues that are at the core of our work as speech and language therapists working with practitioners in early years, and in this chapter we share our journey through these considerations and conundrums. Our ultimate aim is to arrive further down the road of promoting truly thought-provoking, creative and sustained conversations with all children.

We have been working in early years settings in inner-city London with high numbers (70–95%) of children learning English as an additional language (EAL) since 2001. Initially we were part of an innovative education action zone project formed by a group of mainstream schools that were concerned about the level of spoken language in the foundation stage in their local area. This has been found to be reflected nationally, where research has shown that 40–50% of children at school entry have speech, language and communication needs that, if addressed early, will recede (Hartshorne 2006).

The project gave us the opportunity and freedom to experiment with new ideas for service delivery and for ongoing dialogue with early years practitioners. We started by modelling small language groups (up to five children at a time) so as to enable practitioners to put their knowledge of language development into practice by observing children's responses to adult-led activities. This meant that they in turn could identify the children in their settings who needed more support with their communication skills. This was the only way of working that we had experienced at the time and was rooted in a more traditional speech and language therapy model, where the adult sets the context and topic of communication, based on children's language 'needs'. These 'needs' are identified using a health service-based 'deficit' model of assessment and intervention where 'gaps' in the language development of individual children are worked on.

We realised fairly early that structured groups were limited in scope, in terms of children's true involvement and meaningful learning. They were not easy for practitioners to sustain in mainstream nursery and reception classes, due to the high staff ratios needed for the groups. In addition, the techniques introduced were difficult to generalise to wider, more child-initiated classroom activities.

At about this time, we became aware of a swell of related research in the fields of both speech and language therapy and early years education. More and more studies emphasised the importance of child-led activities to inform the observation and planning cycle (Sylva et al. 2004). Similarly, a wealth of studies has highlighted that adults have a vital role to play in adjusting the language environment and in developing children's personal, social, emotional and communication skills by using 'responsive' or 'helpful' interaction strategies. As Michael Rosen, the former Children's Laureate, states in the foreword to *Every Child a Talker: Guidance for Consultants* (DCSF 2008: 1), how we speak to children is 'crucial for how young children develop their powers of thinking and understanding … At the same time, it is how they get to feel good about themselves. The two things are intertwined – feeling good about yourself and feeling confident enough to develop your thinking and understanding.'

The research has proved the effectiveness of specific responsive interaction strategies for children's language development in controlled studies. The strategies can be grouped according to the three main areas of encouraging children to start conversations and make connections, maintaining and encouraging balanced conversations, and adults modelling vocabulary and extending the topic to scaffold children's language skills. The specific techniques (Girolametto et al. 2008; Weitzman and Greenberg 2002) are as follows.

Strategies to encourage children to initiate and engage in conversation

By observing, waiting and listening, being face to face and following the child's lead (by imitating, interpreting, commenting) practitioners can respond appropriately to the child's topic of interest.

Interaction-promoting strategies to encourage extended balanced conversations

By using a variety of questions to encourage conversations and balancing comments and questions and modelling (i.e. by linking words to objects and actions), practitioners can listen carefully to the children, tailor responses to their interests and not dominate the conversation.

Language modelling strategies to build children's language skills as well as their emergent literacy knowledge

By using a variety of words, expanding on what the child says and extending the topic by modelling language out of the 'here and now', practitioners can scaffold children's language development.

We felt that working directly on adult–child interaction should be our focus and was the way we could make a lasting and measurable difference to children's language development. To this end we developed the 'Talking Together' programme. 'Talking Together' uses self-reflection and video feedback so that practitioners can work on how they interact both in relation to individual children and in small groups.

The 'Talking Together' programme

'Talking Together' was based on well-established existing speech and language therapy programmes looking at the interactions between parents and children (Kelman and Schneider 1994; Pepper and Weitzman 2004) and practitioners and children (Greenberg and Weitzman 2002). It was built around the three groups of positive interaction strategies highlighted above. The programme involved taking a five-minute baseline video of each practitioner interacting with a chosen child in everyday classroom activities. Six hours of in-service training about adult–child interaction for all the practitioners and five to six weekly video feedback sessions with pairs of practitioners and two speech and language therapists were provided. It was run in four settings with 22 practitioners in total (two mainstream school nurseries and two nursery schools). The baseline and final videos of each participant were evaluated on three quantitative measures adapted from Law et al. (1999). The measures, relating to the three broad groups of strategies, were as follows:

- Child initiations versus adult initiations ('initiation' was defined as a look, an action or word/words that start or move the interaction forward).
- Comments (on the child's focus of attention) versus questions on the part of the adult.
- Number of adult responses to child initiations versus number of adult responses which were contingent on child's initiations (i.e. responses which had less than one second's delay, where accurate vocabulary was modelled and where there was repetition/expansion on the same topic).
  By the end of the programme 11 out of the 14 children involved were *initiating* conversations a great deal more and 9 out of 14 practitioners were *commenting* much more. Eight out of the 14 practitioners were *asking fewer questions* by the end of the programme (Hayon and Typadi 2004) (see Graph 1 and 2 p. 000).

'Talking Together' emphasised the child's perspective (i.e. the practitioners were following the child's lead, from which all other positive strategies followed) in a way which language groups had not. Its drawback was that this quality intervention was time consuming to deliver. 'Talking Together' also emphasised interaction in everyday routines and in open-ended activities. This, however, meant that there was not a uniform and defined context in which the adult could initially practise the interaction strategies. This made 'Talking Together' challenging for some practitioners.

The 'helicopter' story-telling and story-acting technique

At around this time we were introduced to the 'helicopter' technique by Trisha Lee, the artistic director of a London theatre in education company called MakeBelieveArts, who ran a series of training workshops for early years practitioners in Westminster. Trisha Lee worked closely with the American early years educationalist Vivian Paley, who had developed a curriculum in her kindergarten classes in Chicago, USA, based around children's stories. The technique derives its name from Vivian Paley's book *The Boy Who Would Be A Helicopter'* (Paley 1991). It involves children dictating their stories to an adult or an older child (e.g. a 'buddy') who writes them down exactly as they are said. Later the same day the stories are acted out in front of the whole class, without props.

We felt that the 'helicopter' was an ideal vehicle to 'put interaction into action' in a defined context. It allows adults to practise letting the children lead in a flexible one-to-one situation as well as in the large group during story acting, and relies on adults dedicating time so that they can genuinely listen to children. For these reasons we believed the 'helicopter' could work well in mainstream settings where there were large numbers of children and relatively few adults.

How does the helicopter work?

To describe the helicopter we would like to tell you a story.

It was a Friday morning just before playtime in a reception class. The teacher took out the class's large, gold-covered exercise book. She announced: 'It's time to tell our helicopter stories now', and encouraged children to write their names on the class story-telling list. Some children were already at the small-world table which also frequently became the story-telling table. Akizun was one of the first to tell her story. The teacher was not surprised, as first thing in the morning Akizun, who had been off the previous day, had come into the classroom very excited and wanted to tell the teacher about the party she had been to the day before. At that time the teacher had had to say: 'That's sounds fun. Perhaps you can tell me all about it later, at story-telling time.'

Now the teacher opened the book and Akizun was eager to write her name at the top of the page. The teacher added the date. She smiled and waited expectantly for Akizun to begin. Akizun said: 'My story is called "The Function". It's going to be a long story.' The teacher reminded her that the story could not be more than a page because other children wanted to tell their stories too. If her story was longer, she could continue it on another day. Akizun began:

> When my Mum and me and my sister and my little brother and my Dad camed and brought his car, we all went inside it ...

The teacher repeated the words as she wrote them down. This showed Akizun that she had heard Akizun correctly and also slowed down the pace of Akizun's dictation. Akizun asked the teacher: 'Which one says "Mum"?' The teacher pointed to the written word 'mum' and in this way Akizun saw the link between the spoken and written word made explicit. Akizun carried on:

> and then we ... my Dad, got my auntie and my uncle and my little baby cousin, we all drived to the function.

The teacher repeated Akizun's words without correcting the grammar, as she was aware that if she started to correct grammatical inaccuracy it would be difficult to know where to stop and she would lose the 'poetry' of Akizun's self-expression.

Akizun continued:

> we saw some singing song and the man and the lady singing, and then it was dinner time. It gived us drink and water and then more dance camed, some ladies and man got some fowers.

The teacher repeated 'flowers' correctly. Akizun hesitated and the teacher probed, 'Is there any more?' as she knew she needed to ask questions sparingly. After a pause, Akizun said:

> and then the man gived us fowers and then we had more drinks, then we bought some flowers, then we went home.

The teacher read back the story to Akizun and underlined all the characters. She asked Akizun how many ladies she wanted and clarified who 'us' referred to. Akizun said she wanted seventeen ladies and the teacher suggested that they might need to have fewer because there wouldn't be enough room on the stage for all seventeen children! Akizun agreed to have five ladies and also chose to be herself in her story.

The teacher collected stories from six other children, one more at the small-world table, three in the book corner and two outside. At the end of the morning she prepared for story acting. She knew that stories should be acted out fairly soon after being dictated and always within the same day. Vivian Paley talks about the child giving part of himself when he tells a story – like a gift. To act out the story is to accept the 'gift' and recognise the child's contribution to the classroom.

The teacher found a roll of masking tape and called all the children to the carpet. They sat around the carpet and the teacher marked out a rectangular 'stage' with the tape, big enough for the children to move freely within it. She reminded them that no one should come onto the stage unless invited, and that there should be no touching of other people. The teacher knew that Akizun was still shy in a large group, but because she had been so keen to tell her story, she thought it would be a good one to open the session.

The teacher said: 'now we are going to act out some of our stories' and 'the first story is Akizun's story. Akizun would you like to come and sit next to me? Akizun has chosen to be herself in her story.' Akizun came and sat next to the teacher. The teacher started to read out the story to the next character and the children got up from their places around the stage to act.

The teacher said: 'When my Mum … '

'Can you come and be Mum, Tom?' Tom shook his head and the teacher validated his decision by saying: 'That's OK, we need story listeners too.' She continued: 'Arif, would you like to be Mum?' Arif smiled and immediately got up and went onto the stage. This meant that the helicopter was allowing him to explore themes from different viewpoints (for example, in the 'helicopter' boys can be Mummies and girls can be Action Men). The teacher waited to see how Arif moved as the Mum. When he stood still, the teacher said; 'I wonder how the Mum moves?' When she saw that Arif still wasn't sure how to show being the Mum, she asked Akizun how the Mum might move. The teacher was using the rule of thumb that if the actor is unsure, consult the storyteller, if the storyteller is unsure, then ask the audience. She knew it was important for the adult not to impose our 'grown-up' way of acting on children and to use 'I wonder … ?' questions. Akizun showed Arif how her 'Mum' moved, holding a bag.

The teacher then carried on reading: 'me (that's Akizun), how do you move?' Akizun smiled and stood behind her 'Mum'. The teacher continued reading the story and inviting children from their places in the circle: 'and my sister, and my little brother and my Dad camed, and brought his car, we all went inside it'. The teacher asked Akizun: 'Where would you like the car to be?' Akizun pointed to the corner of the stage and the children all moved there. The teacher continued: 'then we [*sic*], my Dad got my auntie and my uncle and my little baby cousin, we all drived to the function'. The teacher knew it was important to involve the whole audience and asked 'Can we all pretend to drive?' The children all enthusiastically joined in with driving actions and teacher continued: 'We saw some singing song and the man and the lady singing and then it was dinner time. It gived us drink and water and then more dance camed, some ladies and a man got some flowers … '. The teacher said: 'We need five ladies, one, two, three, four, five … Can you come up and be ladies and can you be the man?' She waited for the 'ladies' and 'man' to show giving flowers. She continued: 'and then the man gived us flowers and then we had more drinks then we went home.'

The teacher signalled the end of the story with the phrase: 'And that's the end of Akizun's story. Thank you very much Akizun.' Everyone joined in a round of applause for Akizun and the other actors.

The technique is described by Trisha Lee in detail in the *Helicopter Resource Pack* (MakeBelieveArts, 2002).

Supporting inclusive practice

As speech and language therapists, we were interested not just in introducing the technique into early years settings but also in how it could be used to support inclusive practice and identify and support children with speech and language difficulties. Every child has a story to tell and the 'helicopter' allows all children access to the experience of being listened to, having their story scribed in their own words and acted out in a physical dimension. No child is forced or coerced and every child is respected.

We found that children learning EAL or children with speech, language and communication needs sometimes wanted to 'tell' a story through play because they lacked confidence in expressing themselves verbally and needed vocabulary and grammar explicitly modelled by an adult. This is the 'language modelling or scaffolding' group of interaction strategies that are otherwise not brought into play with the 'helicopter' technique.

Toys or objects can be set out for the child to use. The adult interprets the play, comments on what the child does with the toys and makes this into a story. The process is shown in the video *The Boy Who Could Tell Stories* (Vivian Paley 2001). Another example comes from a Westminster reception teacher who had recently introduced the technique in her classroom. She reported the following interaction when taking a story from a child who had recently arrived in the UK. The teacher had set up a dolls' house to facilitate 'story telling'.

THE CHILD (JAMAL) PICKED UP A BOY DOLL.
TEACHER: Is that Jamal?
(JAMAL NODS ... MOVES 'JAMAL' TO BEDROOM OF DOLL'S HOUSE.)
TEACHER: Jamal in bedroom.
(JAMAL MAKES THE BOY DOLL JUMP.)
TEACHER: Jamal jump.
(JAMAL MAKES THE DOLL JUMP ON THE BED.)
TEACHER: Jump on the bed.
(JAMAL GETS THE MUMMY DOLL AND MAKES IT JUMP ON THE BED.)
TEACHER: Mummy jump on the bed.
(JAMAL MAKES MUMMY DOLL LIE DOWN.)
TEACHER: Mummy lie down.
JAMAL: Finished!

Stories can also be made of a child's utterances when they look at a book with an adult. For example, a little boy, Luigi, aged 4, with severe social communication difficulty, told a story based on his favourite story. He looked through the book and named the pictures: 'cat ... horse ... cow ... sheep ... duck ... quack, quack'. The words were written down as he said them and Luigi nodded his head to indicate agreement. Luigi then acted in the story-acting session later the same afternoon, playing the part of the duck in his own story, and joining in with the actions as part of the audience in the stories of other children. As the weeks progressed this child with severe social communication difficulty was actively included in a whole-group classroom activity.

How we used the technique and measured its impact

We were keen to use the 'helicopter' as a practical means of focusing on interaction strategies within a well-defined context. We visited two private nurseries, one nursery class and five reception classes. Our aim was to introduce the technique and support practitioners in implementing its principles. We also jointly identified an interaction strategy for the practitioner to work on. Each practitioner identified two or three targets from the following.

During story-telling:

- To ask one question at most, e.g. *'What happened next?' 'Have you finished your story?'*

During story-acting:

- To refer back to the child whose story it was for ideas about how to act a given role.
- To wait five seconds for a child to act the role before asking the storyteller or the audience.
- To involve the audience in actions.

All teachers achieved their targets by the end of their blocks. They reported higher levels of confidence in taking stories from children in the classroom and were able to give children learning EAL or less-confident children the time they needed to express themselves. Teachers also reported enhanced skills in leading the story-acting sessions and attributed this to regular opportunities to discuss with the project therapists how to conduct the sessions and how to involve all children. All practitioners were very enthusiastic about continuing to run 'helicopter' sessions.

The following is a practitioner's reflection on how she became aware of her interaction style through the 'helicopter' technique.

Lee was one of the youngest children in reception – he would be five during the August holidays. During the early spring term, we had concerns about his spoken language and his concentration skills. Although English was his first language, his family had different heritage languages and his grandfather, who had minimal spoken English, had recently come to stay, taking over a lot of the after-school care of Lee.

We had recently begun our 'helicopter' stories with this class and most children were on only their second story. Interest was high and we had made a list of children who wanted to tell a story and were working through this daily. Lee had been invited to tell a story several times but had always turned this down – although he had joined in some of the acting out of stories. Today, he asked to have his name put on the list and waited patiently but persistently, listening as others told their stories.

When it was his turn, Lee came and sat down next to me. He sat expressionless and I thought he might not know how to begin his story. I looked at him expectantly and waited … and waited. After a few moments, I said aloud, 'I wonder how your story will begin?' I then sat on my hands, bit my lips and waited … and waited. I managed not to butt in again and Lee began to tell me his story. At first he dictated one word at a time, slowly and monotonously – no expression on his face or in his voice. I wrote down his words, repeating them as I did so. After the first sentence, the words gradually gained momentum until they were pouring out of his mouth so fast I could barely keep up with him; excitement burst into his voice and flooded into eyes as he continued his story. I had never seen him so involved, animated or fluent in his speech.

Lee listened, enraptured, with a smile floating on his face, as I read back his story to him. He chose the character he wanted to play and went off to find his friends. Later that day we acted out his story around the stage – he was delighted.

The helicopter stories helped me to see Lee in a different light. I learned not to be so quick to prompt or encourage verbally and practised a 'listening' face and pose.

In addition to our focus on adult's interaction skills, we were also interested in developing a system to capture change in the children's confidence and communication skills. In consultation with education colleagues, we devised a termly observation sheet to record the children's progress through the Foundation Stage in the areas of confidence and imagination in acting, turn taking, attention and listening, and in narrative skills such as providing a sequence of story events, statement of character, place and time, and use of connectives and book language. This form incorporated many of the Early Learning Goals from the areas of Personal and Social Education (PSE), Communication Language and Literacy (CLL), Creative Development and Physical Development. It was used as a baseline and final measure and proved to be a very practical means of measuring children's progress over time.

In total, 24 children were targeted (between three and five in each setting). Nineteen of the 24 were learning English as an additional language, and of these, 18 were also deemed to be lacking in confidence in using English at school. In addition, two children had specific language impairment; one had suspected communication disorder and one had a diagnosis of Autistic Spectrum Disorder (all EAL).

Many children made substantial gains. Of the individual PSE measures (confidence to try new activities, level of support needed for acting out stories, attention level and ability to wait for their turn) children made most progress in turn taking (i.e. being aware of and waiting for their turn to act), followed by confidence to participate and ability to listen. Similarly, all target children (except three who remained the same) made progress on at least one of the language measures (sequence of story events, use of connectives, statement of character, place and time, use of book language). Dramatic increases in length of story told were also very common.

The two children with specific language impairment made identifiable gains in PSE skills on a par with all the other targeted children using this inclusive, whole-class technique. Language gains were more variable, depending on the individual child.

Graphs showing the children's progress on PSE and language measures are provided in Figure 3 and 4.

The following are pen portraits of how the 'helicopter' was embraced by different children in one reception class over a six-week period.

MARIAM (4 years, 11 months) was a little girl who was becoming very interested in reading and writing. She came to tell a story under the whiteboard. The therapist commented on the date (21 June) and that it was the day with the most light, and that it was also very sunny. Mariam remembered the words written on the whiteboard earlier by the teacher: 'today it is hot and sunny', and wanted to read and re-read these to herself. She kept saying the word 'cold' for 'hot' but eventually read the sentence

Talking together

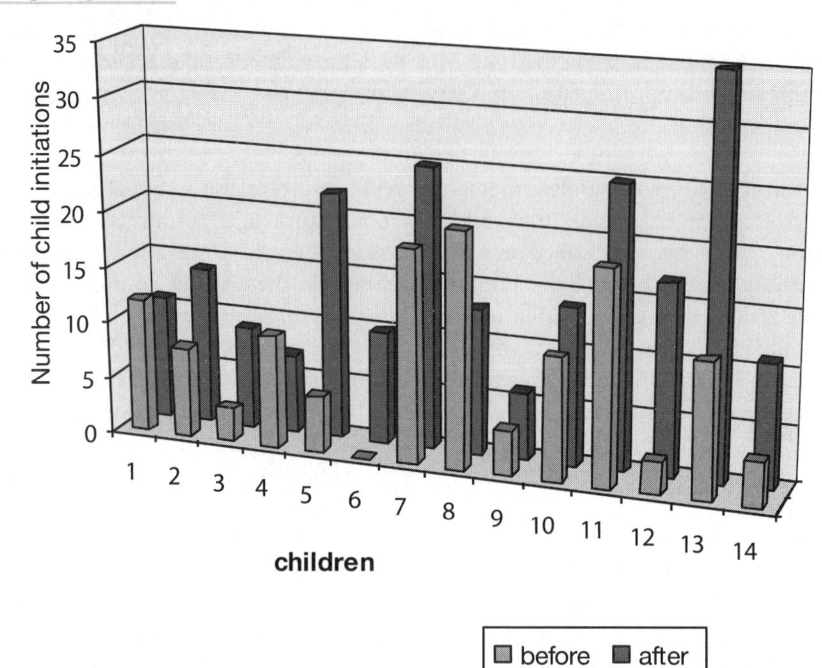

Figure 1

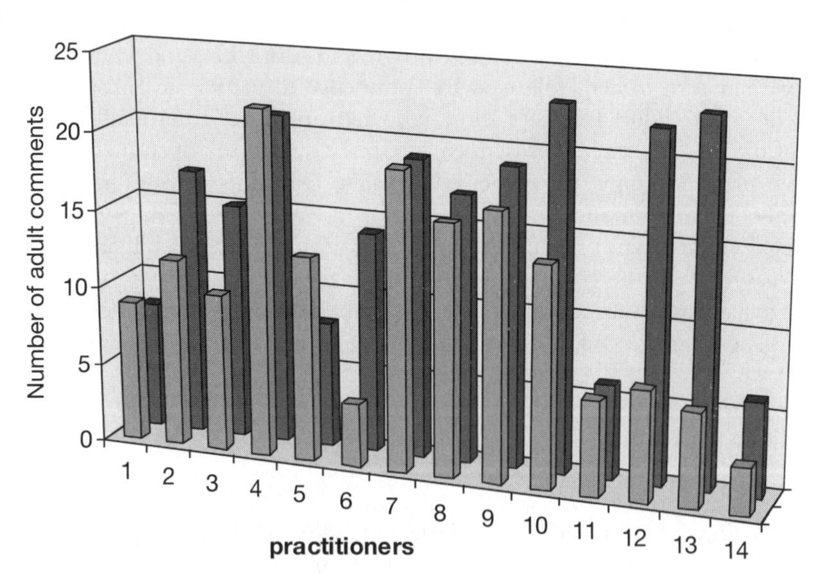

Figure 2

PSE measures

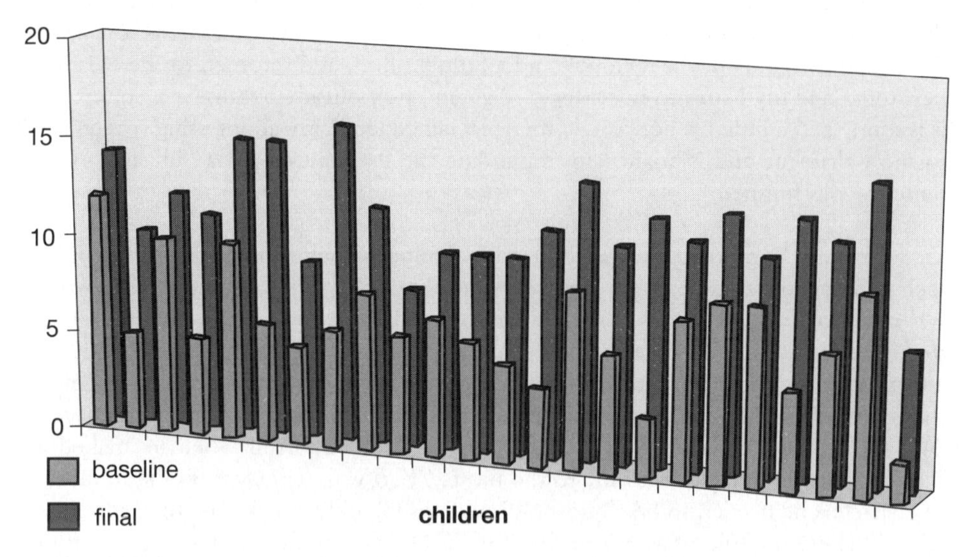

Figure 3 Children's PSE Score in Baseline Final Story Acting Session

Language measures

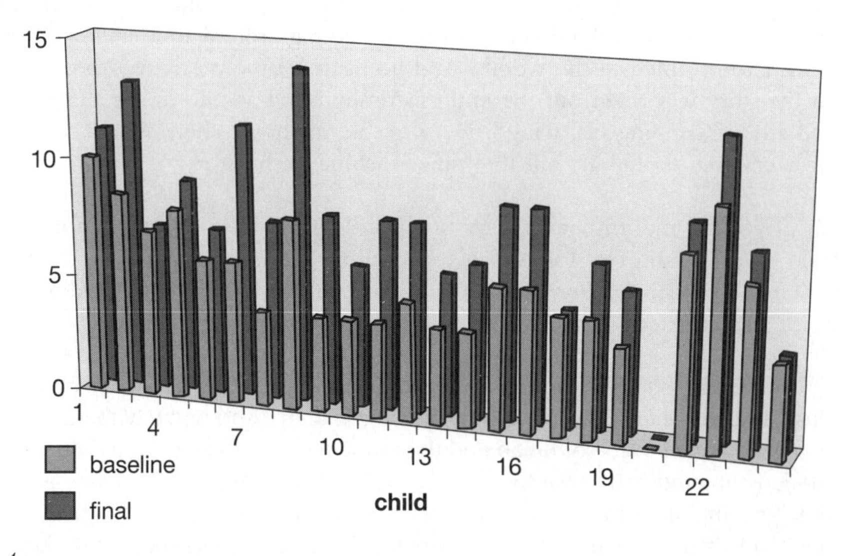

Figure 4

correctly and asked if the teacher could come and hear her read the words. This was done and the teacher congratulated her on her reading. Then Mariam began her story with the same words: 'Today it is sunny and a little bit hot', and was fascinated to see the words written down as she spoke them. She repeated variations of weather descriptions, e.g. 'Today it is cloudy and a little bit hot', and returned to the weather in her story, 'and my Mum to my sister say "go and play outside because it is sunny, today it is sunny and a little bit hot"'. The therapist talked explicitly about using speech marks to show dialogue and Mariam kept reminding the therapist to put a 'full stop' when a sentence was finished.

KARL (5 years, 2 months) was a child with significant behavioural difficulties. The technique appeared to engage him very successfully on the therapist's initial visit, when he told a story to his teacher after seeing the technique demonstrated. This story was in fact the only one acted out. Karl told an impressive story about an astronaut who 'waked up and went out and saw it was something strange. 'Cause that's why there was his work outside and the buildings were in the wrong places. And the zoo was open, the gate, and the lions were out. And when he maked a time machine he travelled in time to the future.' Karl was very clear on the numbers of characters he needed to be clouds (6), buildings (3) and to make the time machine (5), and chose the role of astronaut for himself. He was confident in acting the story out and the therapist was surprised, after meeting him over this single afternoon, that this child was well known to the early years advisory teacher team in Westminster. In subsequent story-acting sessions, Karl found it hard always to sit still, with hands to himself, but despite needing to be given 'time out' in a later session, tried to edge himself back into the acting. He continued to decline cross-gender roles (e.g. to be a 'Mummy'). He spontaneously told a second, shorter story to the therapist later on: 'There was two dragons flying and two lions running around in a circle and there was a man who camed in the woods. And he made a time machine. And that's it.' When the story was acted out, he enthusiastically acted as one of the dragons and jumped around flapping his 'wings'. He was able to show where woods would be and how children should act out the 'time machine' in his story.

MISBAH (5 years, 9 months) was a very bright little girl who spoke Persian at home. She told two sophisticated stories two weeks after, with an introduction, event and resolution which her teacher noted she could probably write herself. Her stories were:

> One day there was an old lady and an old man. They live in a cottage (just pretend). They didn't have any food and money. And one day there was a lady. She give to the old man and the old lady some money. And then the old lady and old man went to buy some food. And they eat their dinner and they give their son some food. And they was happy. And they was rich. And they say thank you to the lady. And the lady say 'Welcome'. And they growed some flowers and then a butterfly came and sat on the flowers. The end.

Once upon a time there was a little bear. She was a girl. And there was a daddy and a mummy. And the little bear, she wants to go to ballet. She was sad. She really really want to go to ballet and she asked her mum to go to ballet. And her mummy say 'no'. And (mum) she said 'You can't go to ballet because you have to get 7 years old to learn'. And she was very sad. And she say 'Why I can't go? My sister can go'. And then she became 7 and she's mum say you could go. And then she was very happy.

Misbah was confident to direct the other children when her stories were acted out, due to the teacher's excellent referring back and waiting. At the end of the acting out of the second story, she spontaneously gave a joyful pirouette to symbolise her happiness at being able to dance.

BILLY (5 years, 3 months) was a boy who had not focused in class on group activities or spoken very much in the classroom throughout the year. He was very eager however to tell his stories during the sessions and told stories in each session, each covering an A4 side of paper (i.e. around 120 words). Two stories were acted out and Billy was enthusiastic about showing the other children how to act the roles in his story, e.g. a yellow tissue. His teacher commented how the sessions had made a big difference to Billy's confidence in the classroom.

The 'helicopter', as has been documented by Vivian Paley (2001) and Trisha Lee (2002), brings substantial benefits for the children and adults involved.

Benefits for children

We truly learn what the interests and preoccupations of the children are and thus their home world is allowed to enter school. Children's stories cover an enormous range of topics, often mixing real events and fantasy with themes ranging from the mundane to the momentous, from contemplating one's foot while swimming underwater, to the birth of a sibling, and occasionally domestic violence. Children may also choose to make everyone laugh with a cheeky version of a well-known tale or nursery rhyme. Examples of stories illustrating this diversity of themes are given below.

> I went on the bus. I went on the bus to Hyde Park and I played on the swing. And I went to the shop and I got sweeties and I got a lollipop too. I got crisps. And then I got another lollipop. I took a bus home. And then I ate all my things at home.
>
> Once upon a time there was a wall and Humpty Dumpty climbed it. And Humpty had a great fall. And all the king's horses and all the king's men, couldn't put Humpty together again. And somebody strong came to help him and fix it. And they all lived happily ever again. And that's the end.
>
> Baa baa black sheep, had a great fall, that's it.

> Once upon a time there was a man. He went to the shops. He saw a little girl by her own. She couldn't find her mummy. She went to the Harrow Road. She bought some sweeties with the man. She went to get some ice cream. A little boy came. They was in love. They been married and the man saw them and the boy and the girl went home. And they hold hands and when it was night time, they saw a girl with another boy. The girl hold the other girl's hand. They went to the shop by themselves. They got lots and lots of money. They've got 51 million. They've got lots and lots of hundreds of sweets and we saw a dog and a cat. That's the end. They lived happily ever after.

> Humpty sat on the house. He was round like an egg so everybody eat him. Finished.

> Once upon a time there was a girl called Lucy Blue. She never played with any colours except blue. She wore blue and one day she was playing with her toys when she needed a bath. She made a fuss. Her Mum put her to bed without any story. There was a thunderstorm. She cried half of the night. Soon the thunderstorm stopped. And she went to sleep. She got up the next morning. She went to her Mum's room, she woke her Mum up and her Mum screamed. She was covered in blue. She hurried to the bathroom but that's the end of my story.

> Once upon a time there was a dolly. I went to my bedroom. I saw my doll. When I was sleeping it was gone. I went outside. I saw a duck in the mud. When I go back home, I saw my Mum's television but I put it on and then the electricity went and then the people came. The people put it back on. I went outside. I played on the slide. When I went back home, there was lots and lots of rain and it was thunder. I went to sleep. I saw a big smash of thunder, I saw a biggest ghost ever. He is nearly eating me. My Mummy came. She saw the ghost, she done the loudest scream. She made it go away. I was sleeping. I had a Barbie dream. When I was waking up, I went to school. I played with my friends. And that's the end.

Children use stories as a way of conquering their fears, 'making sense of their lives' and exploring the world, as the story above about the storm indicates. The 'helicopter' permits children to have a voice about serious issues, e.g. guns, good and bad, superheroes, power (Fahy 2003 and MakeBelieveArts 2003). This gives practitioners a valuable insight into areas most important to children and can inform planning. Children have given the following reasons for liking the 'helicopter':

> We can write what characters we like in it and we can write Spiderman or Batman or Superman.
>
> (Boy aged 5)

> Because it's fun and everyone gets a turn.
>
> (Girl aged 5)

The use of drama in the technique encourages dialogue between children and practitioners and enables children to communicate ideas. We have noticed that shy children become more confident in acting out a role because there is no pressure to speak or act, they can act as part of the audience, and they know that their ideas and actions will always be accepted.

The 'helicopter's' structure neatly gives children just what they need in terms of their own language development. Thus, a child dictating a story consisting of three or four words gets each of these emphasised on acting out, to reinforce meaning. A child dictating a whole story, however, helps to 'direct', and sees a longer and more complex sequence of events come to life.

Another of the 'helicopter's' interesting and less obvious facets is that it fosters a sense of a group, or what Vivian Paley calls 'a community of storytelling'. Children learn from each other. At first, all the stories are similar and the children copy one another but it does not take long for them to yearn to be different. They may also repeat the same story over and over again, and this helps to establish connections between the known and unknown for the child.

The technique also enables children to develop their attention and listening skills when they listen to and join in with others' stories as part of a large group. Children and adults listen with rapt attention because they don't know what the next story will be about and what will happen next. In addition, children practise their turn-taking skills in a meaningful and motivating context (through using the story list at story telling, getting up to act in turn around the circle and waiting for other children to act with their own ideas in story acting).

We have also found that the 'helicopter' supports children's learning of new vocabulary, as it allows them to make the link between actions and spoken words. The 'helicopter' technique also emphasises the uniqueness of each child's imagination. For example, when one of the therapists was leading a story-acting session, a little girl had the line 'twinkle, twinkle little star' in her story. The little boy who was the star was unsure of how it should be represented. The adult wanted to impose her idea that the star could be represented with arms and legs stretched out wide, but was conscious that she needed to refer back to the storyteller. The storyteller confidently went round to the little boy, adjusted his hand as though his thumb and index finger were holding a star and the boy patiently held his hand in this position for the duration of the story.

Children also have the opportunity to develop their role-playing and pretending skills when, for example, in a single session, they may be asked to represent such diverse ideas as a 'castle', how a grandmother or a tiger might move, or how to show making a sandwich.

The technique has been observed to foster negotiation skills between the children; in one reception class a child was waiting impatiently for his friend to finish his story and urged, 'Come on, finish your story!' His friend replied, 'I'll put you in my story, what do you want to be?'

Finally, the 'helicopter' provides children with a meaningful reason for attempting to write their names on the storytelling list and eventually, for some of the children, an incentive to write and read their own stories. In one of the reception classes, one boy was always reluctant to participate in any writing activities taking place in the classroom. However, he was always very eager to tell stories and one day, some months later, to the joy of his teacher, he pretended to scribe the therapist's and another child's stories.

Benefits for adults

The 'helicopter' also has a number of important advantages for the adults involved. It provides a context that encourages practitioners to reflect on their interactions with children, 'suspend the teacherly agenda' and follow the children's lead. Adults need to show trust in children, actively listen to them and encourage them to elaborate by using time and silence. In addition, adults have to become more aware of their own body language and their use of praise and questions so that rich and genuine speaking and listening opportunities are created. Finally, there is scope for adults to comment on and interpret a child's play with toys and objects and to make this information a 'story' if necessary for children learning EAL or for those with specific language difficulties.

The 'helicopter' lends itself to a school environment, and particularly to a reception class, because the whole group needs to come together for the acting. This is crucial and necessary because, as Vivian Paley puts it, 'the life of the class is in its stories'. The 'helicopter' binds a class together (Paley 1987) and allows the children to share thoughts, borrow ideas and add their own insights. The 'helicopter' can also be used in schools throughout Key Stage One to boost children's confidence and creativity. Older children acting as 'buddies' from higher up the school have been used successfully in a number of London schools to scribe the stories and lead the story-acting sessions (MakeBelieveArts 2003). The skills this bestows on the older children, in terms of social confidence in leading the acting and the literacy skills of the real and meaningful story-taking task, cannot be exaggerated.

What makes the technique particularly attractive to practitioners is that it does not need detailed prior planning or organisation of resources. However, for practitioners to develop professionally, planning of peer observation is required.

What I like about the 'helicopter': a speech and language therapist's perspective

Story gathering

During this phase I made the following observations.

Because the interaction was totally led by the child, I felt a sense of anticipation about what he or she would say (as the subject matter could be anything) and also about how long the story would be – anything from a few words, to several sentences, to a page of transcription.

The stories gave fascinating insights into the child's home or other key locations and experiences in their life: a real voyage of discovery not only for me as listener-scribe but also the child as they explored and developed their sense of imaginative expression.

The children each responded positively to having one-to-one adult attention, and an attentive listening scribe gave space for the child's creativity to develop – the freedom and confidence of the child's thoughts grew with the story.

I initially needed extra concentration to avoid anticipating or prompting the child's thoughts in any way and to ensure I recorded exactly what the child said – in this sense the scribe is very much in an active listening role.

It was important to tell the child clearly that the story stops at the end of the page. It was also key to remember to read the story back at the end, to ask the child who they wished to play and to find out how many children would be needed to represent core elements of the story, such as a location or character. While it was not the end of the world if this aspect was forgotten, including it reduced potential confusion and also saved time.

Acting in the story-circle

My immediate impression was how inclusive this therapy tool is – whatever the child's communicative ability, confidence, background or personality. The stories are as varied as the individual children participating, but as the children gather and sit in the story-circle each is considered equal. There is no hierarchy.

The assignment of roles was excellent. Essentially, only the 'author' may choose what role or part to play – apart from this, everyone else goes by turn. This reduces the possibility of confident children taking the limelight. I loved the way 'helicopter' broke down boundaries and perceived roles; for example, girls can take on traditional male roles (e.g. Superman, or a prince) and boys female ones. Because of the number and variety of roles a child may take over the course of acting out the whole class's stories, children gain an increased awareness of how others might feel 'being in someone else's shoes'.

There is plenty of scope to develop the group's understanding of a new character or characteristic. For example a child may be a giant or a dog, but what feelings or expression does this character have? How does it move? It is vital for the adult narrating the story to do it in such a way that the key words are identified and developed. For example, running on a sandy beach – how does it feel? Or sound? Thus vocabulary development is another almost inevitable spin-off. I also really liked the way the element of location was an opportunity for acting (so for example, a number of children could be used to represent the castle, house or whatever the story might require).

The most positive experience for me from 'helicopter' was seeing children blossom in confidence over the single session and even more so over a period of time using this therapy tool. One particular child was too shy to put his hand up in the first story he saw acted, but by the third one was so involved and excited that he was straining to catch the teacher's eye and his hand was waving wildly in the air. This therapy tool also enabled children to work through less-positive experiences in a safe environment and in a structured way; for example, one little boy had observed a police raid.

I was impressed by 'helicopter's' flexible framework, which easily adapts to the needs and abilities of both the individuals involved and the group as a whole. Specific targets for individual children can be set over the weeks it is used. It is a wonderful vehicle to develop the children's enthusiasm and channel their imagination, as well as enabling them to apply everyday experiences in a story context. 'Helicopter' has clearly defined parameters but the children feel freedom within them.

(Personal communication)

Conclusion

We have found the 'helicopter' to be a potent, practical, measurable and enjoyable tool for increasing creative communication in classrooms. It emphasises children's autonomy and readily builds confidence. In terms of the groups of interaction strategies outlined earlier, however, it has a glaring gap – for it does not draw on the language-modelling group of interaction strategies (except when toys or objects are manipulated). It is these strategies that allow adults to interpret, comment on and scaffold children's language within the interaction, leading to a true 'conversation'.

This is where the Talking Table developed by Fleur Griffiths has completed the pieces of our positive interaction jigsaw, providing a practical technique that emphasises all three groups of positive interaction strategies. We have used the Talking Table as a complementary intervention to the 'helicopter', often as a precursor, as it lends itself to working with younger children and builds language they can later use in 'helicopter' stories. We have used similar measures of adults' and children's progress for both techniques.

We have introduced the Talking Table into eight settings (private and voluntary nurseries, and mainstream nurseries and reception classes), usually for blocks of six to eight weekly sessions, with great success.

The Talking Table gives the practitioners involved a classroom technique that they know leads to talk from all the children and where children with less well-developed language skills can practise them in a safe, fun and multi-modal context. This can only boost their self-esteem, confidence and capacity for learning.

The 'helicopter' and Talking Table have many similarities, but also important differences. Both provide an excellent framework for adults to practise positive interaction strategies, both have the creation of stories at their core and both emphasise the link between the spoken and written word (to varying extents).

Their differences lie in the nature of the 'conversation' generated. In the Talking Table, a conversation is built within the interaction through the use of the objects, since the adult needs to use the third group of strategies – the language-modelling techniques of repeating, interpreting or adding to what a child says – before this is reflected back for the conversation to continue. In this way a story is jointly created. The 'helicopter' places its focus on letting the child lead and accepting that lead unreservedly. A child thus creates a story herself and the adult receives it. The 'helicopter' also leads to a 'conversation' between adults and children taking place. The conversation, however, is in the sense that the adult builds in planning on the themes expressed by the child in their stories.

A final attraction of the 'helicopter' is that it provides a practical and flexible framework, allowing both one-to-one and whole-class work. It compels adults truly to listen to children and accept their ideas within a large classroom.

Because they are similar yet also so different, we will continue to offer both the 'helicopter' and the Talking Table to settings we visit.

Our journey along the road of promoting creative conversations with young children in early years settings has been fascinating and challenging. With the help of the 'helicopter' and the Talking Table in particular, we feel we can certainly revisit, and have answers for, the questions asked at the beginning of the chapter.

Both techniques encourage children to speak more, and more creatively, in the classroom, based as they are on experiences and preoccupations from the child's home world. Both can successfully be used and adopted to include children learning EAL or those with specific language difficulties. Both allow children to make connections with and learn from each other in terms of language, ideas and themes. Finally, with the aid of practical descriptive observation sheets, practitioners can identify, support and track children with language difficulties.

Our journey has taken us, as speech and language therapists, away from our roots in health into a new world of early years education that emphasises the whole group over the individual and positive strengths over 'gaps'. We continue to be amazed and in awe of the meanings we can jointly build when we allow children and 'tuned-in' adults to engage freely in creative conversations.

Take a tip

Practise letting the child lead. Try offering to write down exactly what a child wants to say without comment or correction. Try out the positive interaction strategies suggested here and reflect on the consequences of Observe, Wait, Listen (OWLing).

Reading and resources

DCSF (2008) *Every Child A Talker* (ECAT) Programme, London: DCSF.

Fahy, C. (2003) *Foundation Stage Story Telling and Story Acting booklet*, Westminster: LA.

Girolametto, L. and Weitzman, E. (2002) 'Language facilitation in child care settings: a social-interactionist perspective', in *Enhancing Caregiver Language Facilitation in Child Care Settings*, proceedings from the Symposium, 18 October, Toronto, Canada: The Hanen Centre.

Girolametto, L., Weitzman, E. and Greenberg, J. (2008) *Learning Language and Loving It*, Hanen Program for Early Childhood Educators/Teachers, Research Summary, Toronto, Canada: The Hanen Centre.

Griffiths, F. (2006) 'Two tips from the Talking Table', in Talking Point, www.ican.org.uk.

——(2005) 'The art of conversation', *Times Educational Supplement*/Practitioner, 11 February, 6–7.

Hartshorne, M. (2006) *The Cost to the Nation of Children's Poor Communication*, London: London Borough of Bromley.

Hayon, K. and Typadi, E. (2004) 'Talking together in the foundation stage', *Bulletin of the Royal College of Speech and Language Therapists*, April, 8–9.

Kelman, E. and Schneider, C. (1994) 'Parent–child interaction: an alternative approach to the management of children's language difficulties', *Child Language Teaching and Therapy*, 10 (1), 81–94.

Law, J., Barnett, G. and Kot, A. (1999) 'Coding parent/child interaction as a clinical outcome: a research note', *Child Language Teaching and Therapy,* 15 (3), 261–75

Lee, T. (2002) *Helicopter Resource Pack*, London: MakeBelieveArts.

Lee, T. (dir.) (2002) *Monsters and Superheroes, The Helicopter Technique Storytelling and Story Acting in the Classroom*, a documentary about the innovative Peer Group Education work of MakeBelieveArts, London: MakeBelieveArts.

MakeBelieveArts (2003) *Newsletter*, **6** (Spring Term) MakeBelieveArts, London, www.make-believearts.co.uk.

Paley, V. (2001) *The Boy Who Could Tell Stories*, VHS Tape, Muncie, IN: Ball State University.

——(1991) *The Boy Who Would Be A Helicopter*, Cambridge, MA and London: Harvard University Press.

—— (1987) *Wally's Stories: Conversations in the Kindergarten*, Cambridge, MA: Harvard University Press.

——(1986) 'On listening to what the children say', *Harvard Educational Review*, 56 (2), 122–31.

Pepper, J. and Weitzman, E. (2004) *It Takes Two To Talk*, Toronto, Canada: The Hanen Centre.

Sylva, K., Melhuish, E.C., Sammons, P., Siraj-Blatchford, I. and Taggart, B. (2004) *The Effective Provision of Preschool Education (EPPE) Project*, Technical Paper 12: The Final Report: Effective Pre-School Education, London: DfES/Institute of Education, University of London.

Weitzman, E. and Greenberg, J. (2002) *Learning Language and Loving It: a guide to promoting children's social, language and literacy development in early childhood settings*, 2nd edition, Toronto, Canada: The Hanen Centre.

The power of colour and light

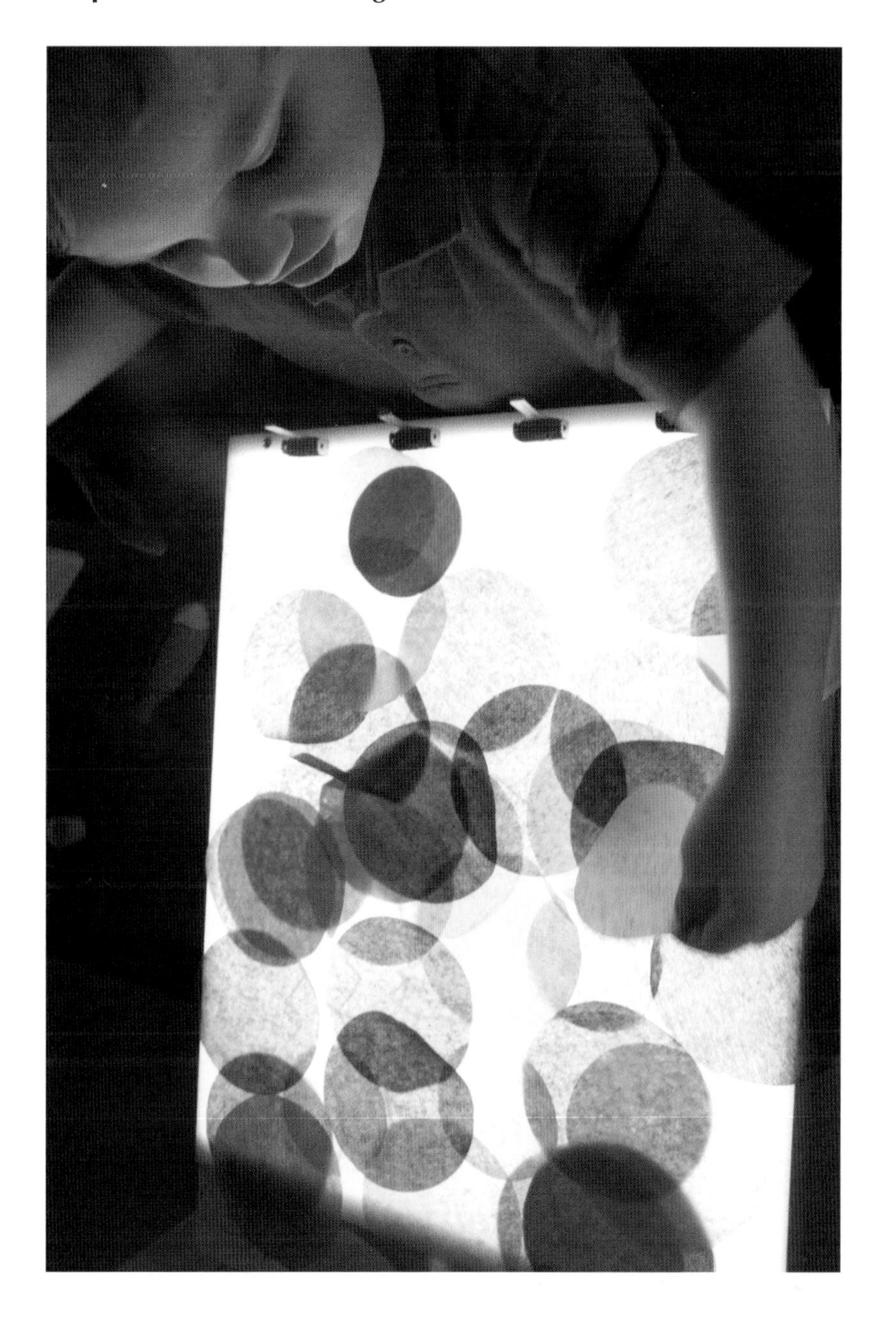

Matthew loves enclosing and enveloping , and uses the light table to develop his ideas
'That's all my pattern, and this is the spider's bed.
I like spiders.'

Monkchester Family Centre

Materials in dialogue

Intelligent materials are rich with possibilities. They invite exploration and reinvention. These open-ended materials provide the vital ingredients in the life of an idea.

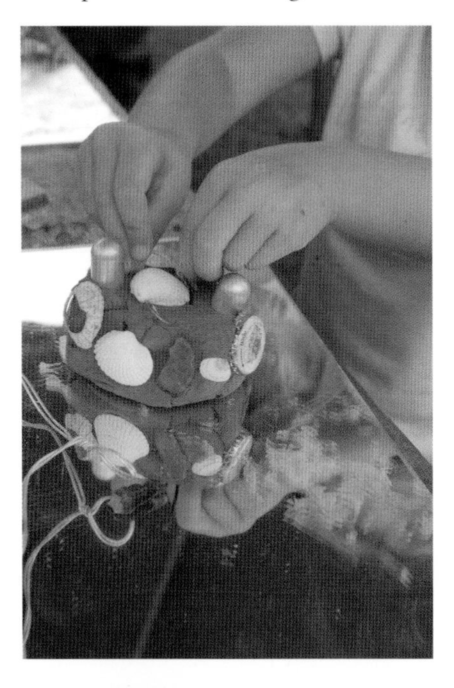

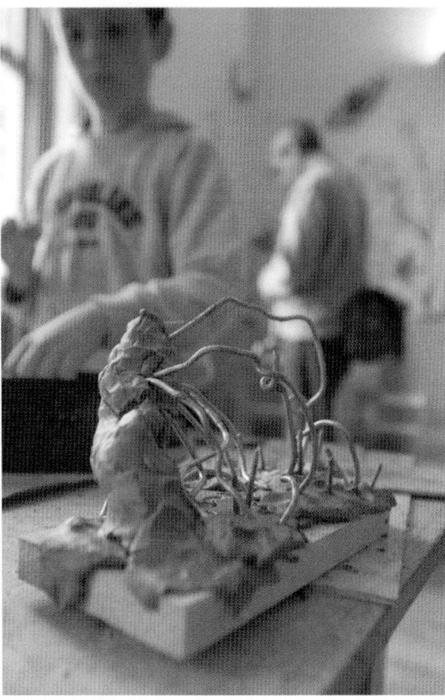

The House of Objects Creative Recycling Centre North Tyneside

Time and space to reinvent uses for open-ended materials

A group of boys sort through the materials and an idea emerges.
'A car!'
'We need some wire.'
'I make wheels.'
Soon a problem occurs.
'The wheels don't fit.'
'Use them beer things!'
'Why don't we make a coach?'
'That's it!'

They all agree and redouble their efforts. Jack runs off and finds different diameter tubes.
'What's that for?'
'That's the engine.'
'Yes, this, put this in here, this is for the engine.'

'I like building stuff. I'm just using wood.
It's a rocket car! It's rocket boosters!
The car is going to be massive!
It's tricky now. It's got a chimney.
Not even one piece nearly fell, not even them wheels and they roll!
I'm going to use all of this box of wood!'

The House of Objects
Creative Recycling Centre
North Tyneside

Enriched Environments

An outdoor area that inspires and supports creative play and exploration with natural materials

Houghton Community Nursery School

Leona has an idea.
She begins to cast a spell, using her hands to weave magic.
'That's pink magic. It can magic people into frogs.
The frogs turn into ghosts, green and pink ones.'
Leona looks at the notes to see that her spell is written down correctly.
She writes her name carefully next to the spell.
Leeonaa.

'I can see the orange!'
'It's cracking!'
'It goin bigger!'
'Careful, and don't touch it!
'I can't see anything, just smoke.
'I can hear the dinosaur. The dinosaur might burn his face on the fire.'

Houghton Community Nursery School

The enabling culture of the classroom, the mirrored wall, props nearby and music that the children control — these elements add layers of meaning to the children's play and dance.

Naomi's mirror dance.

Atkinson Road Nursery

The Drama of Art

Large scale painting on the vertical, with a harmonious colour palette and tools which engage the whole body in mark-making.

Monchester Family Centre

Collaborative drawings as a tool for story-telling reflection.

Gabrielle 'It's Neve dancing

Matthew 'That's the ghost. I catch ghosts everywhere. I seen them as well. I catch them at nursery.'

Hylton Red House Nursery School

Oliver's Paintings Tell a Story

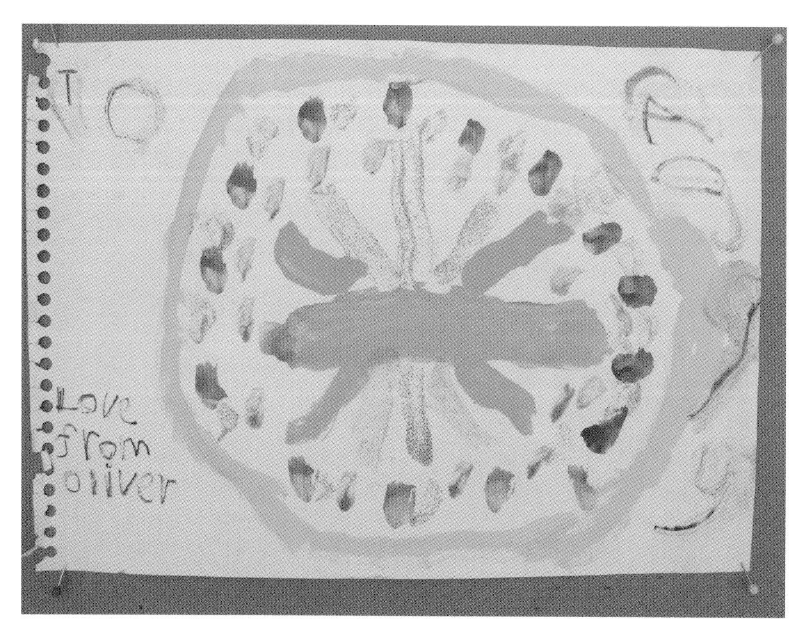

1. *'The grey big bit in the middle is the middle of the universe and the rest are the spiral arms of the galaxies'* (Oliver at home, age four)

2: *'The rocket is at the bottom firing smoke and fire. Around it is all stars. The blue is a spire with burners and radars. There are white wings and a face to scare other ships away. The blue is how it goes into warp speed. The crosses are the phasors. The other crosses are to make it look cool and the red blobs are the extra boosters'.* (Oliver at home age 4)

Paintings Tell a Story

3: *'These are the flowers and this is Aggie. This is her new walking stick and that's her favourite flower. That is the giant Sequoia. And those spots are Aggie's eyes. There is the blue of the sky and the sun. (Oliver at home, age3)*

4: *'Here is a green giraffe with a few trees he's nibbling the grass and trees... The pink is the shiny sky like a sun going to sleep and there is a bird (orange) coming so close you cannot see the other part of the tree'.* (Oliver, at Home age 3)

Paintings Tell a Story

5: *'This is me and Emily and our shopping list. There are two bricks holding the tent down. There are apples and oranges and posters to let you know what it is. There's loads of rain, billions of rain and black scary emperor clouds. (Star Wars theme). The rain is like the signs of the emperor. On the car the windscreen wipers are working.'* (Oliver's School trip to the local market age 5)

6: *'This blue is the sky. There are two suns. This is a really big rainbow. There are chunks of grass and flowers to help feed the rabbits and the snails. I did it all red 'cos I knew the colours but I did it red to make it beautiful.'* (Oliver at home, age 4)

Paintings Tell a Story

The Desert and the Egg

'Here is the desert and the camel. You can't see the camel' (both painted in yellow on the left). *'The white shape with a yellow centre is 'a fried egg'!* Lee smiled at his joke.

The Desert and the North Pole

Lee painted a large red patch which was the 'desert' and the pink oval he explained was the North Pole. Then he pointed to the rest of the painting and said, *'And this is the whole world'*.

Drama of Sound

Listening Intently

Gabrielle listens intently to the sound of the flute.
'It was slowly.'
She listens again *'It's soft.'*

Hylton Red House Nursery School

Drama of Sound

It makes different sounds when you do this (pressing the buttons)

Hylton Red House Nursery School

Drama of Sound

Hylton Red House Nursery School

Drama of Sound

With every pause in the music the children make shapes, changing their poses, experimenting; sometimes alone, sometimes in pairs, or creating a sculptural group of three then four then five.

Hylton Red House Nursery School

Drama of Sound

The children are excited, they begin to move and dance to the music .The shadow screen allows them to see their shapes in a very graphic way.

The children are full of ideas from shape-making in previous sessions.

Gabrielle 'I'm a mermaid.'

Paul makes outstretched arms.

'He's a angel!'

The shape-making becomes a performance, full of drama.

Hylton Red House Nursery School

Music making

Music round a cloth

Stephanie Brandon

Our team of musicians at The Sage, Gateshead, works to encourage the people who care for little children in their range of environments to be confident in singing together, to create a joyful atmosphere. We work directly with the children alongside parents, carers, volunteers, practitioners and teachers. We do this by inviting them to see and share some of the things we do together with the children.

We want children to explore and understand the relationships between noise and sounds; sounds and music; music and noise. Our approach is to introduce and reinforce, through experience and demonstration, many different ways to enable them to do this.

We want them to see the value of a greeting song where we sing everyone's names to acknowledge who is there. In this way we make sure we all know each other's names and set the tone for the environment as a singing setting. We also want to demonstrate the value of song in itself as a tool to develop memory, encourage language development and give everyone the wonderful feeling of exhilaration which comes with singing. Language is based on communication through rhythms and sounds. Activities that encourage awareness of these aspects of communication aid development.

We show ways of exploring song-making ideas through a range of concrete stimuli. Puppets that mysteriously come out of bags, pictures, teddy bears, pebbles, leaves: all these and more can be put into a song at the drop of a hat, if you practise enough. Children's needs for developmental movement play or simply to move vigorously can be met with music: dance/pulse/rhythm activities entailing jumping, wriggling, rolling in time to song, chant or music give the opportunity to practise and develop rhythmical awareness. At the same time their creative imaginations are engaged.

We show how to encourage gross motor play through lycra and parachute activities with songs, chants and rhythms. Around our circular cloth, we spend time with children exploring the sounds made by a range of instruments and other sound-making objects. Children will focus for an astonishingly long time on exploration and discussion, stories about where things come from, taking their turn, learning to organise sounds to make music. In my experience they don't really want to make noise – they want to know how to make the noise be musical. Dynamics and pitch play, linked to storytelling, animals, movements, seasons: all enable children to find more ways of using their creative imagination to make music. In this sort of learning environment they also learn a wide range of social skills – how to value everyone's contribution, how not to put down anyone's idea, how to make sure things are fair and we all get a turn – which enable the music-making experience to be a shared and exciting one.

In a regular music session led by musicians, we have to gather all the ideas together and work with energy and variety in a concentrated period of time. We hope that the parents, carers and practitioners we work with can see that this is how to demonstrate ideas but that, most importantly, all the ideas can be taken and used in a range of contexts across the day and in the future, rather than contained in one session.

We believe that the threads of song, rhythm and music should be woven into every area of the child's day. We like to see song used to call attention, give information or reminders; to reinforce children's learning, engagement in and memory of activities. Pulse awareness using the whole body can be brought into every transition time to engage the whole body and brain for a short, intense period while we wait to move on. Children need opportunities for free exploration of anything that makes sound, not just musical instruments, and to share what they have learned with each other. But most importantly, children – everyone in fact – need to have the opportunity to sing for joy.

The integration of music and song in these ways provides a supportive framework within which children can learn to develop their creativity in very positive and cooperative ways. It gives parents and practitioners who may not see themselves as musically able the opportunity to see how they can be part of this framework and learn with their children. It gives more children the opportunity to develop their awareness of sounds and their listening skills, which will impact on their learning of language.

It enables all of us to create learning environments that have at their heart joyful, meaningful and creative interactions.

Musical movers sessions

Creative ideas for using movement with young children

Angela Foley

One of my children refused to get out of bed to go to nursery one morning because she was too tired. Under pressure to get ready and out, I could feel my tension rising and an edge creeping into my voice. Then, before I was able to get into stern mother mode, the song 'I jumped out of bed in the morning' popped into my mind. This song involves a list of things that need doing in the morning – stretching, dressing etc. – along with the positive refrain 'I hope it's a very nice day'. I started singing it and my daughter joined in. Before we knew where we were we were ready, smiling and going off to nursery with a lot of good feeling between us – and singing the song probably took less time than an argument or tantrum.

When I go into schools I say I'm not a musician, I'm a human being who loves music and the more you hear it the more musical you become and it becomes as natural to you as breathing.

In conversation

This chapter marks my own creative journey from home into work and it endorses the idea that children and adults make this journey together, as the following statement declares:

> Young people's creative abilities are most likely to be developed in an atmosphere in which teachers' creative abilities are properly engaged.
>
> (NACCCE 1999: 90)

Although I am not a trained musician, my musical skills have developed as I have worked in this area and I feel I have become more creative in the process. I now feel able to go into schools and share ways of using music and movement with young children and their carers.

The song that popped into my head that morning saved me and my daughter from a battle and helped us to feel good. But encouraging laughter and fun is not only about making people feel good and enjoying themselves. Psychological studies provide clear evidence of the importance of positive experiences in enhancing the well-being of young children. Positive emotional experiences are important in encouraging development in babies and young children (Gerhardt 2004) and positive emotions help us build up reserves and resilience for the future (Seligman 2003). It is not just fun to have fun; it helps us to learn. There is also research evidence that the experience of music can result in people 'becoming more positive, more alert and more focused in the present', which are states of mind that help learning (Juslin and Sloboda 2001).

I have also adopted ideas from interactive music therapy. Interactive music develops play, sensory exploration, motor skills and a learner's ability to communicate (Corke 2002). It emphasises the importance of relationships within the social context of learning. The facilitator acts as a more able partner, encouraging learning and communication through interactions or conversations.

The qualities needed to run music sessions with young children are those qualities of communication needed for all early years work: to be enthusiastic; to be willing to give it a go and not to take oneself too seriously; to be accepting; to be sensitive and affirmative; and to believe in the value of what you are doing. Very few people are tone deaf and unable to sing, and for most people their perception of not being able to sing comes from lack of experience or confidence. This is best overcome by actually singing. Singing is good for us; it can be done by anyone; it also costs nothing. It is too good a resource not to use it often and in many different ways with young children.

I worked recently with a nursery nurse who was not confident in her own singing ability. However, as I watched her work, I was captivated by her enthusiasm, her facial expressions, her encouragement and her very positive interactions with the parents and children in the group. She felt she could not sing, but she was so skilled a communicator that whether she could sing well or not was not an issue.

> When we sing we tend to become more interesting, not necessarily because of our beautiful singing, but because as we sing our facial expressions, body language and voice patterns tend to change.
>
> (Corke 2002: 13)

My own creative journey

Since 1998 I have worked in a variety of early years settings using music with young children and their carers. I came into this work almost by chance. I took time out from my work as an educational psychologist to be at home with my children and I was fascinated to watch the way music supported their development. As babies, they would spontaneously move to music, and, from being very young, loved to have repeated-action songs sung to them. They enjoyed the actions, the repetition of language, the fun – the peek-a-boo, the bounces, the tickles, the playfulness, the fact that Mum and Dad were giving them positive, warm attention. They giggled and bounced when they were sung to and their reactions made me laugh and feel good, and encouraged me to continue: so our early conversations developed. Not all our musical interactions were energetic and arousing. The children loved to be calmed with song: they could be distracted on long journeys by sing-songs; quiet knee-bounces kept them occupied in doctors' waiting-rooms; and singing calmly and gently to them would have a calming effect on me. As in any conversation, we were all changed by the interactions.

Music also worked directly on me. When I was having a bad day and felt at the end of my tether, I realised that singing a song could change my mood and my interaction with my child. Sometimes, in the middle of toddler chaos, just sitting down and listening to some music that made me feel good could recharge my batteries and give the respite that I needed. I realised how helpful music could be to so many aspects of parenting, to children's development and to the developing relationship between children and carers.

When my eldest child started school, I set up a pre-school music and movement group in a local church hall, mainly for the fun involved in doing it, but also because I was interested from a professional perspective to see whether what I had learned about my own children and music was applicable to other children and their carers. This was the first step in my own creative journey: I had a hunch about something I was interested in; I wanted to give it a try; I used my imagination to work out the possibilities; I then riskily started out without having a clear end in view or knowing where the process would lead.

Often parents who attended the group would tell me that they felt the sessions gave them permission to play with their children, to watch their children and to respond to the children's communications. I tried to use 'hands-on' activities that encouraged interactions between parents and their children. Parents picked up on the messages their children were giving them – messages for 'more' before children could actually say the word, or messages to stop an action or to give a cuddle. We were also amazed at how creative young children could be, as they showed us their movement ideas by dancing to music.

After developing this group and running it for some time, I was invited to help set up a pre-school music group for children with special needs and their carers. I worked as an educational psychologist alongside occupational therapists and physiotherapists, using music to support the children's development and the interaction between children and carers. It was a creative time for me and for others involved: we tried out various activities until we found a format that worked for us but that was constantly evolving as the needs of the children and parents changed. We received feedback from parents about how much they enjoyed the musical play, enjoyed seeing their children develop while having fun, and about the way that the music, singing and group support could lift their own spirits. These were parents whose experiences often involved hospital visits, anxiety about their children's development, fighting for resources, and they talked about the pleasure they got from the positive experiences the group gave them.

Since then I have been involved in running groups in a number of settings – specialist and inclusive. What I have learned from this work has confirmed my experiences with my own children: that working with music and young children can be motivating, soothing, uplifting, fun, and at times challenging. It can aid children's development and can change the interaction between children and carers in a positive way. It can also provide a wonderful opportunity for adults and children to learn from each other and to make a creative journey together.

One mother came into the session feeling very low and tired and with very negative feelings towards her toddler. At the end of singing and musical fun, she said she was going out feeling much more positive about herself and her child and looking forward to the day ahead. Another mother came week after week; her son sat on her knee and appeared not to join in. One day she told me that, as soon as they got home, he would put his soft toys in a circle on the floor and hold a music session, with himself leading the activities. Watching her son lead his group was obviously a source of pleasure, amusement and joy to her.

These are everyday, small-scale events and interactions, but it is the small-scale events and interactions that are the stuff of the lives of most of us. And these events carry powerful emotional significance in children's development and in the development of relationships.

My creative journey and the conversations I have had on that journey have made me more able to trust the learning process. I believe it is immeasurably important that we offer children more opportunities to be imaginative, expressive and creative. Every time I work with a group we are together producing something original with our interactions and ideas. NACCCE (1991) defines creativity as 'imaginative activity fashioned so as to produce outcomes that are original and of value'. Certainly I agree about *originality* and *value*, but not about 'products'; the creative conversations I am interested in fostering are more about *process* than a finished product.

Music as communication

The main aim of my sessions is to use music as a tool for communication. I use props – scarves, puppets, drums, etc. – to increase the interest value of the communication, to provide multi-sensory opportunities, to stimulate the children's ideas and to provide them with materials to express their own creativity. I am also hoping to communicate to children acceptance and respect for who they are and the ideas they have.

Communication is two-way and I am looking always for the ways in which the children are communicating back to me. Their messages can be very clear – laughter, obvious enjoyment and sense of fun. Children can also communicate negative feelings, dislike or distress, and I have to respond to this. For example, in one session one of the children appeared restless and uninterested. He was given the drum to lead a stop/start game, and quickly became involved. He played the drum while the rest of us patted our knees. When he wanted us to stop he put up one hand. He led the game superbly and then settled into the activity as the other children in the group took turns to be the leader. I am looking for non-verbal signals and trying to respond to these. Sometimes I will ask children to offer me an action to fit a song. Some children will very confidently share their ideas, but often one child will look at the floor while tapping his foot or shaking his body, or another will shyly make a small movement. If I feel that the child can deal with the attention, I will let the group know about the tap or shake or small movement, and we will use that action in the song. I want to communicate to children that they are important as members of the group, and activities are structured so that all children, whatever their ability or confidence, feel able to join in with at least some of the session.

I try to communicate that the children's contributions, no matter how small, are valued. The sessions are not about praising successful learning and good singing, but about giving children a positive group experience, where they feel valued and able to participate.

My sessions are planned, but there has to be enough space in the sessions to allow for the ideas and feelings the children bring with them, if our conversations are to be creative, genuine and meaningful. That is one of the exciting things about creative conversations with children – we start them without knowing where they will end.

Musical movers sessions

What do I actually do with young children?

I run structured sessions, lasting about 30–40 minutes with groups of children and their carers. Most children can sustain attention for that length of time if sessions are kept interesting and motivating. I prefer to work with groups of around 10–12 children, or fewer if possible, so that activities can be focused and so that I can be aware of every child during the sessions. All sessions are inclusive. There needs to be a balance of activities; there is often a fine line between stimulating and over-stimulating children. A mix of familiar and new activities can develop children's confidence and at the same time challenge them to learn new things. There needs to be a balance between sitting and moving, being calm and energised, using bodies and using equipment, in order to keep the sessions moving and the children engaged. I have run sessions that have become fraught and, in my reflections at the end, I have realised that I have introduced too many new ideas and pieces of equipment at once. Working with young children – and indeed most group work – involves monitoring the pace and the flow of energy within the group.

Although it is important to expect good behaviour and attention, I don't always wait until everyone is sitting quietly and watching me before I start. In schools and nurseries a lot of time and energy can be spent on control issues: waiting for the perfect group, the very straight line. I find that if I do something engaging the children will notice and become involved. Throughout the sessions I use positive behaviour management, and laughter; praising children for desirable behaviour leads to a much more positive atmosphere in the group than constantly chiding for little things.

There are differences in the ways I run the sessions, depending on the age and developmental stage of the children, but I follow a structure in the sessions that can be adapted accordingly.

Structuring the session

Having a structure to follow acts as an aid to planning and gives some consistency across sessions. Children love the security of knowing what is coming next. Within a familiar pattern, children can improvise. They have leads and starting points from which to develop their own ideas.

In general, I plan a mix from nine types of section, with the group and the length of session in mind. I usually don't use all the sections in every session.

The particular songs and activities that I mention within each section are ones that work for me, ones that I like and am enthusiastic about. Sessions work best if the group facilitators find songs/materials that fit the aims/ideas in each section and that they are also enthusiastic about.

1. Welcome time

A visual cue coming out of a bag can let the children know the session is about to begin. I use a guitar, but puppets or drums could be the cue. Adding sound to sight signals immediately that we are using all our senses. A gathering song is used to call the children together and to mark the beginning of the session.

A song made up to a well-known tune could be something like:

Now it's time for music time, music time, music time,
Now it's time for music time and we're ready now

– to the tune of 'London Bridge is falling down'.
I often use a gathering song (Corke 2002: 71).

I may decide to welcome all the children by name, in order to acknowledge their value and importance to the group. Naming songs like the 'Hello' song are good for this. Encouraging children to wave in response to their name involves everyone, even those who initially don't want to sing.

2. Warm ups

Warm ups encourage participation, imagination and the physical pleasure of movement.

I begin by talking through some gentle massage movements – getting children to rub their own head, arms, tummy, back, legs, face and ears. I then get them to stretch, shake, jump, wiggle etc., adjusting the degree of difficulty in actions to the abilities within the group, and then invite children to suggest actions that they think will help their bodies to warm up. Communicating that it is good to be creative can be challenging; children can be very creative in the shapes and actions their bodies can produce, although at times the line between being creative and being daring and dangerous can be fine. One reception group was asked to suggest movements to warm up to. The first child suggested front press-ups, the next child wanted back press-ups, the third child wanted to roll like a sausage, and the fourth child was happy to clap hands.

Warm-up activities can also set the tone of fun in movement. Warm-up songs help the development of body awareness and coordination through, for example, waving, hand clapping or jumping. Language is being given all the time – simple, repetitive language for basic movements and body parts.

Well-known songs such as, 'If you're happy and you know it' can have the children's own actions added. One of my favourite warm-up songs is 'Wake up wake up, give yourself a shake up'. Not only is it fun, physical and very popular with children, it also involves words that give a very positive message about the day that lies ahead.

Warm ups need to be developmentally appropriate, with lots of hand play for younger children or children lacking physical skills. Groups of children and parents/carers can have fun with hand rhymes, e.g. 'Round and round the garden' and 'Tommy Thumb, Tommy Thumb where are you?'

With parent groups I sometimes use massage oil or hand cream with the finger play to encourage a further sensory experience.

3. Vocal warm ups

Vocal warm ups are important in helping children to be aware of their voices, and to be aware of how their voices can work for them without being strained.

My favourite activity, which I use regularly, is to get the children to put a finger in the air, pretend it is a candle on their birthday cake, count to five together and blow out the candle. We do this a few times, pretend to eat the cake and then make a blowing noise with our lips – all ways of using our mouth and facial muscles, and all activities that most children are able to be involved in. The children are also usually keen to describe their favourite birthday cakes.

I will then ask the children if they have brought various voices with them, e.g. 'Have you brought your quiet (loud, deep, cross etc.), voice?'

They are encouraged to respond each time: 'Yes we have, yes we have', using that type of voice. This part of the session pulls the group together and usually encourages lots of laughter as well as making the children aware of ways of using their voices. A conversation can quickly develop with children offering different types of voices, once they feel comfortable with the activity. They ask their friends whether they have brought their happy, grumpy, cross voices. We were challenged recently by a 'giraffe' voice!

Stephen is a child with coordination difficulties and limited language who finds lots of things difficult and for whom I imagine school life may be difficult. He loved the voices game. Each week he would go into peals of contagious laughter when we did this and each week would say: 'Do the laughing voice again'. We all looked forward to Stephen's laughter, and we learned that Stephen had a gift for seeing humour and for making others laugh.

4. Turn taking

Turn-taking activities emphasise the importance of learning in the group situation. This is an opportunity to recognise and acknowledge the importance of others, as well as to learn the conversational rules of joint reference and turn taking.

This is always one of the favourite parts of a session. 'This is the best bit', I heard recently from one child as I brought out the ball for a passing game. I have a large ball with small coloured balls inside it, but this activity could be done with any interesting ball. The children take turns passing a ball to their friends as we sing, to the tune of 'The Mulberry Bush',

Megan is passing to Freddy, and Freddy is passing to Katie

putting in the names of the children in the group. The game ensures that every child is involved in the session. Although I encourage children to say who the ball is going to before they pass it I am constantly looking to see whether it is too threatening for a child to speak in front of the group, and gauging the amount of support the child needs in order to be involved. At the start I say that it is important that every child gets a turn, encouraging social awareness of each other among the group.

I also do turn-taking activities with a large gathering drum or an ocean drum. We start with some hand-shaking activities to relax and loosen up the wrists. Then we talk about different ways to play the drum and pass it round for each child to have a turn. They may just want to touch the drum, or may opt out at first. The ocean drum is very good for reluctant participators. It has tiny balls inside, and the slightest movement produces an effect. It is responsive to the most tentative touch. Children love to lead the conversations with the drum – playing it for others to follow with their clapping or marching.

5. Theme section

I aim to make the theme section as multi-sensory as possible, using puppets, balls, scarves, saris, bean bags, ribbon sticks, survival blankets etc. I use these props to stimulate movement ideas.

Sometimes I give out ribbon sticks or scarves and have some talk and demonstrations from the children about ways they can move with the ribbon sticks. They then have time to move freely with their ribbons before I bring them together to reflect on and show what they have done.

> A group of nursery children, holding ribbon sticks with long ribbons attached, moved around the room to music. One child discovered that the ribbons made a 'crack' sound if they were flicked quickly, and he decided that his ribbon was a firework. Other children near him heard this idea and joined in 'cracking' fireworks. One child told me his ribbon was for catching fish and he kept bringing it over his shoulder and casting it into the water. Another walked along with his ribbon trailing behind him, walking his dog. One child was a ballerina. Other children made circles in the air or on the floor; we had snakes in abundance, and some children simply danced around, enjoying the free movement of the ribbons. The children gave me their ideas as I danced with them. When we came back together one child was really keen to go into the circle to show what he'd done. 'Me now', he said repeatedly, and excitedly showed the shapes he made with his ribbon as he jumped up and down, saying 'Look at me'. I was told later that he rarely spoke. I think the pleasure he was having with the ribbons took away any feelings of self-consciousness that may often have stopped him from speaking. The conversations, both verbal and in ribbon movement, from a child who rarely joined in was one of those magical moments that will stay with me.

We may play a version of Musical Statues. I give the children ribbons or scarves and we sing:

We're going to shake and shake and stop
Shake and shake and shake and stop
Shake and shake and shake and stop
And now we'll shake some more.

(Tune: 'What shall we do with a drunken sailor?')

Another popular theme activity is The Box. I have a lovely, sparkly, lidded box and I put into it items that are connected to the theme, e.g. puppets. I bring out the box and play a start/stop game, patting the box and encouraging the children to clap their hands, and to stop when I stop. This simple game encourages listening and attention and can evoke lots of laughter. Once the game is established I ask children to take their turn leading the clapping. When we have played for a while I act out a song:

Here's a box and here's a lid
I wonder whatever inside it is hid
Open the lid and see what's inside
Out comes a ...

This works well sung slowly to the tune of 'The Muffin Man'. I act rather than sing the song, using lots of gesture, expressions, eye contact to build suspense, interest and anticipation – as I would when telling an interesting story. I tell the story of what I have put in the box, watch, and encourage the children to engage with the story.

6. Movement session

Most activities involve movement of some kind: clapping, swaying, marching and moving to rhythm. However, a specific time for movement can also be included. The importance of movement is partly related to the development of physical and coordination skills, and also because of the recognised role of movement in improving self-esteem, confidence and thinking skills.

A movement section can include gross motor activities, e.g. marching, circle games like Hokey Kokey or Ring o' Roses. Sometimes it will involve moving in response to music, or movement with a large piece of stretchy lycra. The lycra can be used to lift up and down, hide under, bounce things on top of, stretch in and out.

One of my pieces of lycra is blue and white with swirly patterns and makes a lovely sea. A reception group were enjoying making 'fish' swim by bouncing them on the lycra. The children wanted to go under the lycra and make shapes, and they did this in small groups. Those children holding onto the lycra told me what the shapes looked like. They saw sea monsters, mountains, waterfalls, octopus and other sea creatures. The children then decided that they wanted to see who could make the scariest sea monster shapes, so we got lots of angular, pointy sea monsters and lots of lovely conversation.

Bouncing different things on the lycra is much enjoyed. For this activity to work well, children must hold on and keep holding, so it is a good way to emphasise that everyone in the group has an important part to play – the quiet child who only holds on is needed as much as the very confident child who contributes lots of ideas and sings well. We have bounced toys from our theme story to the tune of 'She'll be coming round the mountain'. Lycra bouncing can be seasonal, for example with paper snowflakes, or autumn leaves.

Children enjoy hiding under the lycra. I have heard the Early Years Team at The Sage Gateshead sing to the tune of 'Skip to my Lou':

Where are the children, where are they, (x3)
Where are they today ... Booo.'

Lycra play can be a wonderful stimulus for language. Songs can be made up to suit the actions. To the tune of 'Looby Loo' we have sung many variations:

Here we go in and out/up and down
Gently/quickly/slowly up and down.

The ideas that underpin the lycra activities can be applied with other props. For example, children love my soft parrot and take delight in keeping it flying through the air:

The bird is flying through the air, through the air
The bird is flying, the bird is flying,
The bird is flying through the air.

They enjoy seeing if they can make the bird reach the ceiling. Great fun is also an opportunity for cooperative activity.

Giant scrunchies (available from Jabadao or home made) can also be used for movement and circle activities. Children can think of different ways of moving with the scrunchy, or go into the circle made by the scrunchy and show off their movements. We make up songs to the tune of 'Brown Girl in the Ring':

Freddy's in the ring tra la la la la ...
He's jumping/running/waving/swaying/dancing. ... in the ring.

7. Instrument time

This section gives children the opportunity for hands-on instrument play. Instruments available in most children's centres are percussive and include bells, chimes, tambourines, maracas, pod-shakers, wood-blocks, rain-makers or xylophones. I have some special ethnic instruments, like a *cabassa*, but children often gravitate towards home-made shakers like rice-in-a-bottle. I do not use pitched or blown instruments, and steer away from piercing sounds that can set teeth on edge, like whistles.

With young children the concepts of loud/quiet, fast/slow and high/low are those that I will work on. Activities with instruments aimed at developing concepts are best adult-led. Tunes, for example 'Do you know the Muffin Man?', can be used for songs that match actions, auditory experiences and words.

We can play the instruments ... and this is how they sound
We can play them quietly/loudly/ etc.

More child-led creative ideas may involve playing rhythmical music and getting children to move and play their instruments. Here the emphasis is not on teaching children musical concepts but on getting them to respond to rhythms and experience the pleasure of making music.

Instruments can also be incorporated in stop/start activities to encourage careful listening. For example, one child leads with a loud instrument and others watch and listen, stopping when the leading child stops. A more complex and challenging listening and attention game involves providing a selection of different instruments. One child chooses an instrument, plays it and then puts it down. The second child plays the first instrument, and then chooses another one to play. The third child plays the first, then second instrument and then one of his own choosing. This can be done with about six instruments. I would not do this activity with a group until I had got to know them and I had some sense of who would be confident to try the long memory sequence. Sometimes activities like this give the verbally shy children a chance to succeed, and can show that lack of confidence in using verbal language does not mean lack of ability.

8. Quiet time

For a lot of children life is busy and noisy and opportunities to relax and experience quiet are rare. There is a growing awareness of the importance of quiet times to encourage calmness, to help learning and to encourage self-regulation of mood. Quiet time at the end of a music session is an opportunity for children to experience calm.

With parents and children's groups I encourage parents to cuddle their children – if the children want to be cuddled – and listen to some music. With nursery and reception children I ask the children to lie on the floor and I talk through a short relaxation sequence: getting them to be aware of the breath going in and out of their bodies, or to imagine being on a beach, or a soft cushion. I then play some soothing music and encourage the children to lie still and listen. At the end of the music, I have a very short period of silence. Parents, staff and children often say that this is the best part of the session for them. Children may find it difficult to lie quietly at first, but this is one of those activities that they become more able to do, the more they practise it.

9. Good bye time

It is important to acknowledge the end of the session. I sometimes gather the children together and we recap what they have done, or I invite them to say what they have enjoyed most of all in the session. A goodbye song can be sung or, as the children are leaving:

Well done ... , well done. ...
Well done ... you've done very well,

can be sung to each of them.

'You've forgotten yourself,' said one child to me at the end of the 'well done' song. 'You've also done very well.'

Collecting ideas and materials

I am constantly on the look-out for things that can be used to stimulate ideas, language, games and musical fun.

Over the years that I have been involved in music making with young children, I have attended many workshops, watched many group sessions being run, and delivered many training sessions that involved an exchange of ideas with other facilitators. I have picked up ideas from here, there and everywhere. I have heard songs sung by children and tried to remember them. I have had people sing songs for me that they have picked up somewhere; material has been passed around orally, almost like Chinese whispers. The result is that I do not know where a lot of my material originates from.

There are some good music resources available commercially, a number of which are listed at the end of the chapter. More and more song books come with CDs, which makes material more accessible to those who do not read music. The government's Sing Up campaign, aimed at ensuring singing is at the heart of every primary school child's life, has produced some excellent resources and offers wonderful training opportunities.

The list of useful resources includes some CDs of children's songs. I use CDs like these to learn material myself that I can then teach to children. I *never* put on CDs for children to sing along to. I believe it is better to sing with a not-very-tuneful voice than to use a CD to support group singing; the non-verbal aspects – the smiles, looks, gestures of the live singer – can encourage enthusiasm and involvement in a way that pre-recorded music cannot. I also make up a lot of the songs I use, putting words to well-known tunes.

My props are gathered from many sources: charity shops, my own children, toy shops. I have bought a lot of my equipment, for example the scrunchies, from Jabadao, a National Centre for Movement, Learning and Health. Although its equipment may seem expensive, I have found that it does last well.

Any time, anywhere

The activities described can be used during a nursery/school day, or done by parents/carers at home. Calming music can be used to soothe fractious groups, transition songs can be used to change activity, action songs can be used if a group have not had opportunity for physical play, language can be developed through song, and music can change or create a mood for staff and children.

Rose observes one of Angela's sessions in her nursery and creates a variation as a followup

Angela's session reminded me that the simplest games and songs are timeless in their appeal. I remembered Angela saying that she has the ability to make up words to go with any tune. I used to do this in my early days as a nursery teacher, and again as a parent, but returning to the classroom after a few years I seemed to have forgotten it. The next day was Red Nose day and as we gathered on the carpet I pulled out some funny red items of clothing from a bag. Most children were wearing red, but those who weren't chose something to wear – woolly red socks to wear as gloves, an enormous, teenager's T-shirt, a clown's red wig etc. We began to sing, 'She'll be coming round the mountain'. Angela had used the tune the day before for 'The bird is flying in the sky', so it came to mind. Going round the circle we sang, 'She'll be wearing red trousers when she comes' etc. After the first few turns, with children sitting as we sang about the red clothes they were wearing, the next child got up and, walking to the beat, stepped through the middle of the circle, through a gap between the children and round the back of everyone, returning to sit down as we finished singing her verse. She smiled when I asked, 'Were you coming round the mountain?' After that everyone else followed suit. What a lovely time we had!

Take a tip

Take courage and try singing more through the day. Sing to soothe fractious groups, sing to get children moving to new activities (even to tidying up), sing to accompany physical exercise, sing to introduce new vocabulary and sing to cheer everyone up!

Reading and resources

Clarke, J. and Taylor, H. (2006) 'Turning their ears on … keeping their ears open: Exploring the impact of musical activities on the development of pre-school age children', Youth Music research report in collaboration with Northumbria University, www.bongoclub.org.uk.

Corke, M. (2002) *Approaches to Communication Through Music*, London: David Fulton.

Davies, M. (2003) *Movement and Dance in Early Childhood*, London: Sage.

Gerhardt, S. (2004) *Why Love Matters: how affection shapes a baby's brain*, London and New York: Routledge.

I Jump Out of Bed in the Morning, from Okki Tokki Unga (1994) London: A&C Black.

Jabadao – National Centre for Movement Learning and Health *www.jabadao.org*.

Johnson, Mark and Johnson, Helen (2004) 'Wake up wake up give yourself a shake up', in *Songs for Every Assembly*, Hersham Green: Out of the Ark Music.

Juslin, P.N. and Sloboda, J.A. (2001) *Music and Emotion, Theory and Research*, Oxford: Oxford University Press.

NACCCE (National Advisory Committee on Creative and Cultural Education) (1999) *All Our Futures: creativity,culture and education*, London: Department for Education and Employment.

Seligman, M. (2003) *Authentic Happiness. Using the new positive psychology to realize your potential for lasting fulfilment*, London and Boston, MA: Nicholas Brealey.

Sing Up, The Music Manifesto National Singing Programme *www.singup.org*.

CDs produced by the Early Years Team at The Sage Gateshead, available from lp@thesagegate shead.org.

First for Fabrics – a source of wonderful, multi-coloured, glittering lycra *www.1stforfabrics.co.uk*.

Improvisation

Children making their own music

Ken Patterson

> I love music! I enjoy having a go, singing and playing with friends, experimenting with new instruments and repertoire. I am an improviser.
>
> (In conversation)

This was not always so. As a child in the 1960s I felt tied in knots and confused by my musical education. What was this thing called *music*? I enjoyed singing songs, moving to music and listening to BBC schools' radio: I was excited about expressing myself through music. But quite early on (even in Reception class) I found the approach that was used to 'teach me music' concentrated not upon what I could do but rather upon my mistakes ('that should be a tah tey not two tahs'). It was didactic and aimed at teaching me skills that I might use one day. But it didn't engage me, or encourage me to express myself or feel emotion in, for instance, a musical conversation with others or telling a story with music. Much of the music making was based on the decoding of music from the stave to voice or instrument: percussion charts with coloured crotchets and quavers for tambourine, cymbal and castanet. It seemed as if I was always trying to achieve a musical result that someone else had written for me. The music was not my own. The music was stilted, with no sense of groove or joy.

Approaches to music have improved since my childhood, and certainly there is more fun now to be found in the best practice that I see. But I think the quality of provision is inconsistent. Teachers, assistants, nursery nurses and parents often lack confidence. So many adults 'educators' tell me that they themselves are not 'musical' and they do not feel able to lead music making with their children. I think that this lack of confidence is as a result of negative experiences in their own musical upbringing. Many tell of being ordered to mime in singing classes because they were flat or sharp, and share horror stories of ending up with the tambourine and being denied the drum.

I didn't set out to be a musician, but as a primary teacher I found that skills I had picked up as a teenager (I taught myself how to play chords on the guitar) were always in demand. Now I am a professional musician, writing for theatre companies and running community bands. As a practitioner I have been involved in many exciting projects where we have worked with young and old, often in cross-generational music making and in situations where musical ideas and aspirations have been shared across cultures. When people of different nationalities come together, communicating with words can be a challenge, and it is music that can become the vehicle for expression. These projects have taught me a lot and made me think. Since 2000 and my involvement in the joyous 'Making Music on the Line' I have been exploring the notion of universality in folk and world musics and exactly what it is that 'makes us tick' in musical activity, with a special focus upon 'what makes young children tick'. How can we learn from each other and share approaches that will work towards a consistent provision of engaging, invigorating and challenging music making?

My watershed projects

Making Music on the Line

Making Music on the Line was a millennium educational project sponsored by Folkworks, Channel 4 and Oxfam. I spent a year coordinating it.

Ten professional musicians from five locations on or near the meridian line brought songs, tunes and dances from their own countries and performed them to each other at a 'sharing' in Hexham, Northumberland. Each musician learned three pieces from each place by ear (creating a repertoire of fifteen) then 'played with it', making the music their own.

The musicians travelled home and introduced the music to children in their region, working with teachers and in workshops. So in Shetland (Scotland), Northumberland (England), Gascony (France), Catalonia (Spain) and Ouagadougou (Burkina Faso) there were many large, celebratory events, celebrating this musical conversation where the only common language was music. In all, 10,000 children took part.

The international musicians who toured the regions were struck by the youngsters' universal enthusiasm for all the songs, dances, melodies and drum rhythms, everywhere they went. Evaluations with the musicians and teachers put the success of the project down to a number of factors including:

- encouragement to improvise, play with and invent new music with the original repertoire;
- learning by ear and responding with movement;
- the use of call and response;
- the chance to perform with the originating musicians at celebratory events.

Jazz improvisations

A number of different projects (The Big People Festival, Jazz Building Blocks, Jazz Attack Northumberland with Creative Partnerships) have brought jazz musicians together with children of different ages. The idea has been to explore musical structures, games and activities that are open-ended and will provide opportunities for improvisation and story-telling. Teachers and children have been involved in making up their own music. The process was always more important than product, although celebratory performance for others was often an outcome.

The evidence from all these projects based upon inventing and improvising music tells us what is useful and valid about making music at all ages:

- Children can own their music; it doesn't need to be written for them in order to be valid.
- Children can make choices and decisions spontaneously and have fun.
- Children can experiment to inform their choices.
- As teachers/leaders, we can explore different musical concepts with our children: rhythm, pitch (high and low), dynamics (loud and quiet), timbre (quality of a sound, often linked to the materials that make the sound), tempo (fast and slow) through improvisation.
- As teachers/leaders we can set up game structures with turn taking in circles where we can step back from being performers ourselves and facilitate, observe and support individuals.
- As teachers/leaders we can relish the fun of open-ended music making, not knowing what the music is going to be but appreciating each contribution for its own worth.
- Musical skill grows alongside experimentation and discovery.
- Musical language and expressive language is learned alongside hands-on music making.
- When we express ourselves we feel good, we are exploring aesthetics as well as gaining skills.

What have I learned on my creative journey?

Music is social

One overriding aspect of world music that is universal is its power to bring people together. Music is seen as an expressive, hands-on art form in that it has a social dimension. It invites interaction and 'conversations'.

Finding your own musical voice is important. Participation in music and singing increases our confidence in catalysing musical activity. One key fundamental that I wish to explore here is that when we invent our own music we feel good about ourselves, we work at our own pace, and we tend to follow a natural developmental approach.

A developmental model

Acquiring language and becoming literate takes time. A new baby tangles with all the information it gains through its senses, then starts to utter, manipulate objects and communicate, eventually making marks with crayon and paper, and starting to read.

In the same way, as developing musicians, we should progress down a pathway of listening, singing, experimenting with sound sources, recording what we've invented with simple notations and eventually starting to read. Learning by ear and responding with movement is basic. Our voices, ears, eyes and bodies are ready to respond to and initiate music at an early age. Traditionally (especially in the learning of instruments) this model is interrupted by the premature imposition of teaching the skills of reading notation before child has played a note.

When a child paints we encourage bold use of colour, texture and form. We, as teachers/parents, are full of praise for bright, vigorous, naive images, showing where each individual 'is at'. It's surely the same for music: bold employment of our voices and bodies to create an expression of who we are. Given the right environment, one of encouragement, permission and lack of damaging critical evaluation, children in the early years seize and relish opportunities to be expressive and responsive. But the expectations of many older children and adult listeners, who are surrounded by recorded music on the radio and MP3 players, are high. They are all too demanding and critical in their response to music, and especially their own music. When listening to naive musical performances they have to find ways to understand what is going on.

We need more positive and inclusive ways of leading music

For our children, we adults need to find ways of being positive in our music teaching, engendering a sense of pride and ownership linked to each individual's ability to succeed. We need ways of debunking our own lack of self-belief so that we can be positive models and join in the fun. We can find ways to promote fun and accessibility in music making, ways based upon experimentation and play, using our ears, voice, hands and body to express ourselves through music.

The fear of a 'din' may make leaders shrink from getting instruments out, but we can't expect children to develop musically without a good deal of sound being made. If we merely concentrate upon control and the acquisition of skills (dry tasks around keeping the beat) we never start to explore true musicality. We cannot ignore an individual's need to experiment and play. We, as leaders, have to enable and look for the evidence of full engagement in musical activity: enjoyment, pride, commitment, willingness and excitement about performing for others.

Being confident, turn taking in circles and letting others (children and adults) support the lead, can take the heat off leading. The best activity is fully conversational.

Improvisation is at the centre of young children's music

For me, the lynch pin is improvisation. It is present in most world music, often not taught, but most often encouraged and expected in, for example, African music. It invites experimentation, it promotes the acquisition of skills by imitation and explores an open-ended horizon in which there is always newness and interest to be found. Improvised music tells stories, it makes you want to respond, it is inclusive, it surprises, it engages and it tells you something about the people who are improvising.

Call and response

Key to world music are structures/games which allow us:

- to echo a fellow musician's words, rhythmic pattern, pitch;
- to initiate simple patterns and gain a response;
- to answer a call with a different response (question and answer);
- to ask different questions and expect a set response (solo and choral chant reply).

Developmentally, experiences can be progressive, starting from the simplest patterns where the very youngest can join in.

A 'safe' environment aids successful improvisation

Children thrive musically in an environment which is:

- emotionally positive: where individuals either trust each other or know that they will be supported by both the group and the leader;
- structured to provide activities where everyone is occupied for most of the time, but where small gaps are provided so that individuals can contribute or respond;
- often based on sitting in circles: this gives everyone the same status and sight contact with each other (including adult helpers, parents etc.);
- in space that's not public or prone to interruption, invasion by sound or being overlooked;
- in a space that's acoustically kind;
- structured around 'freedom through limitation', where individual contributions can be small but much valued, or where the element of challenge is not completely open ended;
- based upon taking turns but with a 'let out clause' for those who do not wish to take their turn.

The foundations of open-ended, group music making

The following list provides a template for developing music making at all ages and stages of development:

1. Chants and repetition, with chances for individuals to make choices in the music making
2. Mimicking or mirroring (responding to another individual's lead)
3. The use of call and response to structure the music making
4. The building of a palette or repertoire of rhythms, notes, expressions through call and response conversations between individuals in the group
5. Musical questions and answers
6. Participants 'owning' their own music
7. Participants signalling changes to others (conductors)
8. The use of storytelling: choice of instruments to explore characters, settings (places, weather conditions or transportation)
9. The use of games of chance (like dice games)

Activities for putting the foundations into practice

These activities have been used with many different age groups. They are not ordered here to be progressive, starting with the 'easiest'. Please pick and choose what you feel you could manage as a leader and build your own confidence, if you are a practitioner.

Some may seem too challenging or inappropriate for the developmental age of early years children. As a leader, you will know your own children and will have different expectations of them, depending upon their age and experience. Choose where to start, watch the children's responses carefully and decide where each of them wants to go next. Once children and their leaders feel comfortable with themselves in a 'safe' environment, these activities will work even with the very young. A child's individual commitment to 'having a go' is the main measure of success and to be valued highly. Once a child feels confident and successful, his musical skill will build accordingly.

1. Chants and repetition, with chances for individuals to make choices, inventing actions as a group

Inventing your own actions as a group provides ownership of ideas. Mimicking each other's actions creates a oneness within the group.

The choice element follows the philosophy of making the music your own. It also establishes the sorts of things you can experiment with when improvising in music (dynamics tempo).

Call and response provides an easy way of leading and learning what is a tricky, syncopated rhythm.

CALL	RESPONSE
Shooby dooby doo wah	Shooby dooby doo wah
Shanga langa lang	Shanga langa lang
Shooby doo wah, Baby push the pram	Shooby doo wah, Baby push the pram
That's cool	That's cool
That's free	That's free
One more time	One more time
But make it xxxx like me	But make it xxxxx like me

Invent your own hand jive and pushing pram actions as a group.

Invite individuals, in turn to fill the 'xxxx' section in the last line (loud, quiet, fast, slow, high, low, sad, happy, angry, sleepy, nose held ... and so on). Take turns in the circle to choose when the chant reaches the last line.

2. Mimicking or mirroring, taking turns as leader

Choosing is a fundamental improvisational skill. The group following a lead and working together, adopting the same pulse, is a key to group improvising.

For each of these activities, sit or stand in a circle.

Switch

Children take turns at being the leader. The leader starts with a body sound (e.g. clapping, clicking, rubbing or stamping), most often keeping a pulse.

The rest of the group mimic exactly the leader's sound, attending to every detail.

The leader can change the sound at will, saying 'switch!'

The other children follow.

Delayed Switch

Delayed Switch is a progression that demands independence and concentration. More expert groups can progress to this version of the game, where the child who is leading starts but the group only joins in when the leader says 'switch!' The leader then changes, but the rest have to wait until 'switch!' is said … and so in effect the leader is one sound out of synch with the group.

Blindfold Switch

Blindfold Switch is a listening game that focuses on employing subtlety in generating sounds: loud sounds are generally easy to guess and could be fun for the youngest. The leader says 'Shut your eyes please', and makes a sound of her/his choice. Individuals in the group listen and join in when they think they know the sound and how to make it. The leader says 'Open your eyes please', and everyone gets to see how the sound was made.

Drumsticks: inventing rhythms

Drumsticks explores a simple instrument and invites experimentation with dynamics, tempo, rhythm, timbre (the quality of the sound related to materials: hard/soft, hollow/bright).

Each child has a pair of drumsticks (rolled and sellotaped sheets of newspaper are a cheap alternative, or custom-made sticks of age-matched length made from dowel from a DIY store).

A child as leader starts beating a rhythm on the floor. Everyone else imitates and joins in. The leader can change, initiating a change in the music (e.g. slow pulse, fast pulse, hitting floor, clicking sticks together, quiet/loud, word rhythms) and swaps leadership by pointing to someone else in the circle.

3. The use of call and response to structure the music making

Improvised phrases can be as simple as one clap, two claps or three claps, a mixture of sounds, e.g. 'stamp, clap, stamp', but can become quite complex, including, for example, 'loud, quiet, loud', word rhythms (with syncopation and groove) and 'rests' in the form of nods of the head.

Echoes

Sit or stand in a circle. With body sounds or using sticks, each participant in turn invents a short rhythmic phrase. Each rhythm is echoed by the rest of the group. This activity can be more physical and expressive if children are standing.

More experienced groups can do this to a pulse or backing track. Alternatively, any rhythmic recorded music will do: the challenge is to find the right tempo for everyone to manage with success.

Pitched echoes

A paired activity using instruments. You will need two pitched instruments, e.g. two colour-coded Combi Bells, or colour-coded chime bars.

Child A invents a short rhythmic phrase; child B echoes the same phrase. Then B takes the lead.

4. The building of a repertoire of rhythms in the group

These activities are an extension from call-and-response patterns, like those in Echoes. They help build a group repertoire, a palette of phrases and ideas that can be used as building blocks for improvising rhythms and scat. Jazz improvisers work in this way, gathering a repertoire of phrases that can be fixed together in an endless set of different orders to create new solos.

Scatting

Over a few sessions the children learn or invent a 'Scat Alphabet'. You could use the one below, or at least some of it (depending on age and experience) by call and response led by the teacher/leader.

> **A**bracadabra, **B**oogie woogie woogie, **C**hoo choo choo boogie, **D**o wop sha dooby, **E**h eh eh, **F**andango dango, **G**ing gan gooly gooly, **H**i de Hi de Hi, **I**ppity bipity I, **J**itterbug jitterbug, **K**ool kat kool, **L**ula hula baby, **M**ambo jambo, **N**a na na na na, **O**o bop sha doodle, **P**ip pop paddy wack, **Q**uickly quietly, **R**azzamatazz, **S**hanga langa lang, **T**widdely diddely dee, **U**mpah lumpa, **V**eodeoh doh, **W**elly jelly in your belly, **X**tra xtra read all about it, **Y**ellow mellow, **Z**ippedy doo dah.

Sitting in a circle, invite each child to choose a scat phrase. Each person in the circle chants their chosen phrase and the rest of the group respond by echoing it. Together work out the hands-knees rhythm of the phrase and then see if you can keep it going as you chant the scat.

Dr Jazz

Learn this rap by call and response. Take turns in the circle, inserting a scat phrase in the 1 … 2 … 3 … 4 section.

> *I was feeling kinda lazy, I was feeling kinda blue*
> *I called Dr Jazz and I asked him what to do*
> *He said there ain't no medicine just scat when you can*
> *Take a few words try to make them scan*
> *Jazz attack baby! 1 … 2 … 3 … 4*
> *Jazz attack baby! 1 … 2 … 3 … 4*
> *Jazz attack baby! 1 … 2 … 3 … 4*
> *Jazz attack babe he took my blues away!*

5. Musical questions and answers

This is another natural progression from Echoes. The notion of rhythmic phrases as questions or answers may seem a little abstract, but a repertoire or palette of ideas soon builds for the group, depending upon their age and experience. A sense of musical conversation really seems to build within a group.

Circle conversations: questions and answers

In pairs, children sit or stand beside each other in a group circle. The first person in the circle improvises a rhythmic phrase (the question) and his/her partner answers with another rhythmic phrase. Then the next pair asks a question and gives an answer, and so on round the circle. An answer may share some of the content of the question or may be entirely different from it. In some way it is a response to the question being asked.

Combi Bells: pitched questions and answers

In pairs in a circle. As in 'Pitched Echoes' pairs can use colour-coded bells to make up questions and answers.

Circle conversations: questions and answers with a 'head tune'

In jazz, there is the notion of a 'head tune'. This is a theme that everyone plays, often at the start and finish of a piece and sometimes in between.

Again in pairs, in circle. As a group, choose a scat rhythm: 'Shooby dooby doo wah, a real Kool Kat'. This is chanted or clapped by the whole group to eight beats (1, 2, 3, 4, 5, 6, 7, 8). This is the 'head tune'. Then each pair performs a question and answer: the question to a count of 1, 2, 3, 4, and the answer to a count of 5, 6, 7, 8. After each question and answer the whole group performs the 'head tune' again. And so on around the circle.

6. Participants 'owning' their own music

The language that the teacher/leader uses is important in all these activities.

Use the language of ownership:

- 'Can we hear *your improvisation* again?'
- 'Let's *experiment* with rubbing sounds to *invent* some new phrases for our new improvisation.'
- 'Let's *share* what *we* have made up in our group.'

7. Participants signalling changes to others

In 'Switch' we saw children as leaders choosing sounds in 'follow my leader' style. A musical term for this role is 'conductor'. The conductor shows everyone else what to do. Children love being conductors (so long as they are with friends in a safe, friendly environment). In these activities children leaders take turns at improvising by conducting others in the group.

Conduct a poem

Choose a nursery rhyme that everyone knows or teach a new rhyme by call and response. Teach the children the meaning of two gestures a conductor/leader will use: a raised hand for 'stop'; pointing to the group for 'go'.

The child conductor/leader faces the group of performers. She/he starts the group chanting of the rhyme by pointing and interrupts whenever she/he chooses. The conductor has to learn to signal clearly and not to make changes too quickly.

Keep changing the leader.

As the children become more experienced, try extending the repertoire of gestures the conductor can use. For example:

- hands close together to signal quiet chanting, moving on a gradual scale to wide apart for loudest chanting;
- one hand raised as high as possible for highest voices down to touching the floor for lowest voices;
- speed (tempo) can be signalled by moving the hands like a steam train getting faster or slower.

Conduct instruments

Try the same approach with percussion instruments. Experiment with loud and quiet, fast and slow (high and low will not work).

Try all metal instruments together on one side and other instruments opposite. Use two hands to conduct, one for each group.

Try a number of different instrument groups. Have one conductor for each group. Ask the conductors to listen to the whole ensemble sound as they conduct and respond to it.

8. Storytelling: choice of instruments to explore characters, settings (places, weather conditions and transportation)

Stories provide wonderful contexts for improvised music, whether they be invented tales (e.g. weather stories, journeys), traditional (e.g. Red Riding Hood, Three Billy Goats Gruff) or book-based (e.g. Going on a Bear Hunt, Funnybones).

Choose your story.

Choosing the instruments

You may want to limit the choice of instruments, at first.

Here are three instruments, which one will you choose for the wind blowing? For the rain falling? For the train? For the troll? For the goats trip-trapping? For Red Riding Hood running? For the skeletons?

Invite the child or group to experiment with all three instruments. They have to listen carefully and decide.

Compose

How will you tell your music story? What sorts of sounds do you want to make? How will you start? When will you play loudly? When will you play softly? When will you play fast? When will you play slow? How will it end?

Try out your story music with your story. Practise to see if you think it works.

Performance

Perform your story and music for someone else. Who wants to be storyteller? Who wants to be conductor? Who is going to play the instruments?

Extensions/progressions

Themes: using three tuned bells make up a theme tune for Goldilocks.

- Timbre: what is the sound of the wood block? Hollow, bright, ringing, dull, wooden, metal? Where might it fit in a story?
- Texture: can we mix the sounds together? Which ones?
- Body sounds: can you use only your body/mouth to make the music? Clapping, hitting knees, humming, panting, la-la-ing, blowing raspberries …
- Paper music: what sounds can you invent, using only paper, to accompany your story?

9. Dice games and games of chance

Dice can help us generate musical ideas within game formats that are fun and take the heat off all the decision making.

Foam dice with a sleeve on each face for inserting different colours, pictures, symbols or words are available from educational suppliers.

Clapping animals

Set up a dice with pictures of animals whose names have a different numbers of syllables. Use the children's suggestions and add if necessary: e.g. cat, donkey, elephant, rhinoceros, duck-billed platypus, hedgehog. Show the dice and together clap the syllable rhythm for each animal.

Split into two groups. Group One rolls the dice and claps the rhythm of the name of the animal that appears. Group Two rolls the dice and claps the rhythm of their animal name; Group One continues and then rolls the dice again for a new name and a new rhythm. Group One changes to the new rhythm while Group Two continues, until they roll again for a new rhythm … and so on.

Pick Unifix from a bag

Set up a bag filled with Unifix cubes of two colours, e.g. blue and red.

'Shut your eyes … take out four cubes and make a rod'. With a blue chime bar and a red chime bar invite the children to play their Unifix tune.

Take a tip

Children can invent their own music; it doesn't need to be written for it to be valid. They enjoy making musical choices and decisions spontaneously and have fun while making them. We can all relish the fun of open-ended music making, not knowing what the music is going to be but appreciating each contribution for its own worth. Opportunities for mini performances or celebrations of improvisations and compositions allow us to punctuate, and make positive, the music making.

When we express ourselves we feel good, we are exploring the world of aesthetics as well as gaining skills.

All this works best in classrooms and settings where a devising approach is adopted across the board, whether children are painting, writing, solving problems, designing or making music. It's up to us as leaders to provide situations for young minds to investigate, debate with and mimic each other, making choices and having fun.

Reading and resources

Patterson, K. (ed.) (1992) *New Dances from Newcastle*; new folk dances for primary children devised by 12 groups of children, Newcastle-upon-Tyne: Newcastle-upon-Tyne Local Education Authority.

Patterson, K. (ed.) (2000) *Making Music On the Line: music from five countries on the meridian line*, Gateshead: Folkworks, The Sage Gateshead.

Patterson, K. (ed.) (2004) *Jazz Building Blocks*, children improvising, Gateshead: The Sage Gateshead.

Patterson, K. (ed.) (2004) *Beat the World Drum: Rhythms from Burkina Faso, Iraq and BoomDang Cumbria*, Gateshead: The Sage Gateshead.

Reflections

Fleur Griffiths in conversation with Rose Davies

Rose observes

I wish I were a girl

One blustery but warm autumn day the children were enjoying running around the garden. Leaves were falling from the trees throughout the day and no sooner had we swept a path through the leaves than more were blown along. Some children were collecting leaves in wheelbarrows, others were kicking the leaves or throwing them high and letting them fall on top of them, and some children rolled among the leaves. Another group of children were playing in a shelter made with a tarpaulin stretched across fences. The wind was blowing wildly at times and the children screeched with delight as the tarpaulin blew about, making loud flapping noises. They used some old bracken to make a bonfire and threw on bark chippings. Someone found a thin stick and poked it in the fire, saying he was cooking sausages on the end of a long fork. It felt as if every child in the garden that afternoon was experiencing the essence of autumn.

I noticed a girl, nearly 4 years old, dancing all around the grassed area. She stopped now and then to pick up a leaf and examine it, then dropped it and watched it fall to the ground. As she danced she sang a song. I listened, and recognised the words from a song she had sung one day a few weeks ago when riding a scooter up and down the tarmac area. (On that occasion she had ridden the scooter and sung for 35 minutes.) The words she sang were 'I wish I was a girl, I wish I was a girl.' As she danced past me and glanced at me I smiled and commented on her singing and she sang 'It's me I was singing about'. Then, as she ran down the hill she sang 'I love to run'. Absorbed in her dancing and singing, running to the top of a bank and down again and then up the opposite bank, she continued singing at the top of her voice, in her lilting Scottish accent, for at least 20 minutes. She seemed aware that I was observing her but was unperturbed and so extraordinarily unselfconscious as, most probably, only a child under 5 could be.

Then Rose asks questions

From this point on I have just jotted down questions to which I have no answers. Maybe the story stands alone and doesn't need more analysis? I would welcome comments from any of you.

Was this a conversation? It didn't feel solitary although she wasn't directly communicating with other children, there were others playing individually, in pairs or small groups all around her. Would it have been the same dance without the other children around her?

Does it matter what she means by 'I wish I was a girl'? As with any song, the meaning doesn't have to be literal. She is a girl with a positive sense of self as a girl within her family and at nursery. She has friends and often plays with them, particularly in the sand and in the home corner. But she is equally happy playing on her own.

It seems appropriate to finish on a questioning note. We wonder what is meant by the girl's song and dance in 'I wish I was a girl' above. Is it simply enough for the adult to notice and share the moment with the child? Ursula Kolbe certainly thinks so in the art arena:

> The warmth of your presence in itself gives support. It sustains children as they interact with the world around them, as they play with materials, and create images. A wordless dialogue of exchanged glances and smiles can often be enough.
>
> (Kolbe 2007: 10)

How do we judge whether there is a need for support or extension of learning? We recognise that we can easily spoil a magic moment by being too intrusive and wanting the answers to adult questions which cut across the child's absorption and pleasure.

We are helped to decide on ways forward by reflection and dialogues with our colleagues. Our Dinner Dialogues have the same supportive function. It is not that we seek definitive answers; we want to be alive to complexity and possibility and to make meaning together. Sharing many perspectives makes us wiser to meaning possibilities and more careful about our assumptions and explanations of behaviour.

Thinking about this enigmatic story, you can wonder about explanations rooted in home conditions, psychological factors, social skills. You can wonder whether the girl was solitary because, with her Scottish lilt, she was an outsider in Gateshead. Our adult minds can easily bypass the simpler but deeper understanding of a shared moment.

Sharing this story, 'I wish I was a girl', brought responses:

> It is so good to have your observations. What it brings up for me is the role of the adult in promoting creativity. I think sometimes that a child, aware of your observation, who continues with absorbed self-expression without being self-conscious or inhibited, only needs the unspoken message of your interest and approval. You clearly communicated this. Someone else might have waded in and probed with questions about what being a girl might mean and made it impossible for the child to respond. I wonder whether the dance and song and leaf could come together in

> another art form – perhaps on paper so that the whole experience is enlarged and shared and articulated by the child at some new level.

This story generated many explanations but the most plausible is the most child-centred one:

> I think the girl was sorry for the leaf. She is dancing this autumn day, make-believing she is a twirling leaf and knowing the leaf would rather be a girl, like her happy self.

Reflections on the Early Years Framework

Rose led a discussion about the new framework, which she has to heed on a daily basis. She is able to use it to promote her child-centred practice. She has no quarrel with the underlying principles outlined. The danger would be if readers skipped the philosophical underpinnings and treated the material as a lesson planner. If developmental stages were applied too rigidly, teachers might use age-appropriate yardsticks to judge an individual's progress. It would be a shame if teachers got so caught up in watching children in order to find evidence of stage/level for the record, instead of observing to learn *the child's meanings* and preoccupations. As has famously been said, 'the file doesn't need to know!' Our concern with collecting for individual files can blind us to social interactions – the group dynamic in learning. Although the EYF asserts that all strands are equally important, creativity does come last, and these divides can be artificial boundaries in a *whole-child* experience. It becomes difficult to know what box to record your observation in!

Rose uses post-it notes to capture special moments of learning –creative moments – to give insights to parents, and to wonder what it might mean for the child and how it might determine the next step. These moments – often unnoticed or disregarded – are marked by a child's concentration, excitement, purposefulness.

She feels that what she sees when observing has changed since she has been thinking about creativity. She sees inventiveness in all areas, not just in the *creativity* area. It is an essential part of play in its many forms and she is pleased that the EYF recognises socio-dramatic play within the creativity section.

> Any approach to language and thought that eliminates dramatic play, and its underlying themes of friendship and safety lost and found, ignores the greatest incentive of the creative process.
>
> (Paley 1991: 6)

Reading and resources

Kolbe, U. (2007) *Rapunzel's Supermarket: all about young children and their art*, Byron Bay, Australia: Peppinot Press.

Paley, V. (1991) *The Boy Who Would Be A Helicopter*, Cambridge, MA and London: Harvard University Press.

10 Conversation and the creative self

Making sense of the research

Marion Farmer

This book is concerned to make claims for and to provide examples of practices which illustrate the importance of the dialogic process in fostering collaborative creativity in children. In this review I will attempt to draw together strands from developmental psychology to provide evidence relating to the type of dialogue that fosters creativity and the creative self. My concern will be with conversational and creative processes rather than products and outcomes. Thus I will first consider what we know of the competence of the young child in the early years as a conversational participant. I will then discuss the fostering of creativity in young children through collaborative interactions. I will give evidence relating to collaborative conversations between adult and child which foster perspective taking, the understanding of conversational processes, the understanding of others in the collaborative process, the conversational environment which enables the child to first produce and then elaborate forms of self-expression (most of the evidence will come from research relating to the development of language, narrative, mental representation, pretence and role play, and autobiographical memory). The processes by which self and other are differentiated through attention to the other, monitoring, imitation and co-regulation will also be discussed. In doing so, I will consider evidence relating to, first, the role of adults (or more competent others) in facilitating the creation of the individual's sense of self, their sense of self-agency and self-expression, and second, the adult's role in the fostering of the imagination within cultural parameters (the culture of the classroom, the culture of the school, the culture of the neighbourhood, the culture of the country). Thus the role of the adult in the child's creation of representation of self and other and self-expression through pretence, language, imitation, the development of autobiographical memory, narrative, and visual and auditory representations will be discussed and evidence reviewed. I will attempt to answer such questions as: What do creative conversations require of children? What do they require of adults? What are the consequences for children and adults? What is created?

Conversational development

Children must learn many roles in order to become participants in their socio-cultural milieu. A key role, involved in all aspects of social life, is that of conversational participant. Children must develop the many skills that we take for granted as adults in order to conduct successful conversations. In order to do this they must first be aware of a large body of implicit information on how to conduct a conversation, and then also know how to apply this information to their own conversational contributions. This 'conversational awareness' is necessary for children to comprehend the intended meaning of another speaker and to successfully convey their own messages to others (Siegal 1999). Siegal, a noted researcher in the area of children's cognitive development, has been concerned to show how the ways we speak with children and question them about their experience radically affect the responses we obtain. His researches into this aspect of child development have led him to the conclusion that 'Young children are notoriously unwilling to abandon their traditional social role as a submissive learner whose task is to comply by absorbing information from others' (Siegal 1999: 10). How do children develop their roles as conversationalists?

For clarity's sake let us start with the meaning of the term 'conversation'. Grice (1975), in his seminal work on conversational analysis, suggested that conversations are regulated by the cooperative principle under which 'each participant recognizes ... to some extent a common purpose, or set of purposes' and attempts to make their contributions relevant and satisfactory in terms of quantity (length), quality (validity or truthfulness of content) and manner (clarity of meaning). Grice's principles are seen as giving guidelines that can be used to assist the achieving of harmonious verbal conversation. As we will see, to some extent children in the early years of schooling have a variety of difficulties in complying with these principles. Additionally, it must be noted that, here in this book, many different types of conversational behaviour are described, some verbal, involving speculation and pretence. These conversations are not so much concerned with truthfulness. In fact imaginative contributions may well lay truthfulness aside in favour of possibilities and escape from the 'truth'. Many conversations here are also non-verbal, relying on gestures and sounds, music and bodily movement. Harmoniousness is clearly important, but a definition of conversation that seems relevant to our book is somewhat broader than that assumed by Grice. A fitting definition would seem to be that conversation is a collaborative social interaction involving the exchange of words, gestures, sounds and signs (behaviours, verbal and non-verbal) in order to influence other participants and contribute to a common aim or joint purpose. Under this definition even the smallest gesture, such as pointing, nodding the head, offering a crayon or taking up a relevant position in a group is a contribution to the common purpose.

How do children develop their competency in becoming collaborative conversational participants? The key to any successful collaborative activity and the primary basis for successful conversation is *connectedness*. This requires the ability to take the perspective of others, to imagine their feelings and intentions and to respond appropriately to forward the collaborative aim. The child must be able to take turns appropriately, knowing when to initiate and when to respond. She must be able to connect her contributions to the conversational contributions of others – verbal or non-verbal. She must be able to repair her contribution if it is not understood or is misunderstood. She must be able to time her contribution so that others can discern it and so that it is connected to the contributions of others. The manner in which the contribution is made must make the message clear, whether it is in terms of volume or pronunciation or of visibility of gesture and movement. In order to understand the appropriateness and effects of her contribution, the conversational apprentice has to learn how to infer the mental states of others from their visible behaviours such as facial expressions, movements of eyes and body and vocal changes.

From studies of conversation interactions with young children we have become aware of some of the young child's competences as a non-verbal and verbal conversationalist (see Ninio and Snow 1999 for a review). By the time they start to talk, children show important non-verbal skills such as turn taking, gaze following, pointing and the use of facial expression. Indeed throughout their first year of life children are typically developing the ability to sustain long bouts of well-timed alternations of turn with adults, who play a major facilitatory role in such activities as peek-a-boo, object transfer, give-and-take games. Indeed by the age of 2 the child is aware of turn taking as an important element in conversations; however, with peers the successful turn-taking pattern appears later, by around the age of 3 years. In terms of the conversational function and meanings of their contributions it is evident that by the age of 3 also children are able to use gesture and verbal means for many functions, such as requesting, greeting, transferring objects, acknowledging, answering, protesting, commenting on actions and objects, expressions of feelings including sympathy, offers and sharing, compliance and non-compliance or resistance, stage setting, and pretend games. As outlined above, a major component of development in collaborative conversation is connectedness – making responses related to a previous turn. Observations of conversations between adults and children show that the supplying of connected responses in conversations rises from around 21 per cent at around the age of 2 years to around 46 per cent at around 3 years. Competence in performance with peers is later to develop. A recent study of conversations between mothers and children aged between 2 and 3 years showed that both adults and children relied hugely on repetition/imitation of the other's contribution to maintain the topic of conversation or 'common ground' (Clark and Bernicot 2008). Clark found that mothers repeated what their children said at a rate of 81 times an hour and children repeated their mothers at a rate of 28 times an hour. She suggests that by repeating what someone else has said, the person repeating both acknowledges having heard the other person and identifies the specific information in play. In this case repetition appears to be central to making sure one has understood what the other person intended to communicate. Thus, when interacting with peers the demands of connectedness on both parts mean that young children sometimes fail to maintain a topic. If they do so, they may use devices such as sound echoing or ritualised variation as well as imitation. A reliance on imitative devices for maintaining conversational cohesion decreases from age 2 to age 5 and connectedness with peers gradually improves over the primary school years. The adult's role here in managing conversational continuity and in inducting the conversational apprentices into their role is clear. It is important to emphasise here the centrality of imitation as a conversational device that aids the development of connectedness by allowing the child to make an appropriate conversational contribution. Imitation, partial imitation and imitation with elaboration are all devices that assist the child and adult to create meanings together. Indeed in many contexts imitation has been shown to be a most important item in the toolbox of children in their cultural apprenticeship in life (Hurley et al. 2008). It appears that individual differences in imitation at 2 years of age in normally developing children are mainly due to environmental influences. Parents who imitate and encourage imitation games have children who themselves are more likely to imitate (McEwen et al. 2007).

We must also take into account the effect of group size on the child's ability to participate. It is suggested that with increase in group size managing conversational pragmatics (such as turn taking and connectedness) as well as the demands of following and taking part in a multiparty conversation are too much for young children to manage. Following multiparty conversation makes demands on memory for others' contributions, rapid information processing, monitoring of human speech (with sound attenuation over distance, ambient noise) and discerning the visual cues from a number of participants. Contributing to such conversations is limited by the comprehensibility and volume of their own speech and indeed also by their confidence and feelings of self-efficacy. Henzi et al. (2007) have shown that in natural interaction in the playground, young children aged between 4 and 6 years are conversationally active in clique sizes of two and three and will be involved in groups of up to four (in a group there are members who are not conversationally active).

Creative development

This book, of course, is not solely concerned with verbal conversations; its main focus is *creative* conversations. What is implied here? What do we mean by a creative conversation? What is meant by the term 'creative'?

Anna Craft, who has written extensively in this area (e.g. Chapell et al. 2008; Craft 2003; Craft and Jeffrey 2008), has recently suggested that, within the educational sphere at least, we should be not solely concerned with creativity in its major cultural manifestations as the production of original works and artefacts. In our roles as adults and transmitters of cultural values we should be more concerned with little 'c' creativity – 'the capacity to use imagination, intelligence and self-expression'. In addressing this capacity she suggests that we should attempt to foster young children's resourcefulness and encourage them to consider and make choices among a range of alternative possibilities in all contexts, including play, relationships with others, group work and problem solving across the curriculum, including the expressive art forms. In so doing we will be focusing not simply on creativity within the arts and sciences but on creativity in making choices, considering alternatives and problem solving in all spheres of life. She also suggests that increasingly 'creativity actually belongs in "communities", residing in the "spaces" between individual minds, rather than being sited entirely in the individual. The implications of this stance are that creativity is rooted in a democratic practice of sharing and developing learning and that it is less a result of genius and more of shared ideas' (Craft 2003: 151). Such a suggestion sits well with much of the practitioner work described within this book. Creativity is seen not as an individual expressive production, unrelated to the contributions of others, but as a shared production, building upon previous experience, suggestions and collaborations.

Considering these ideas about creativity, the definition of a conversation and the examples given in this book, we may define a creative conversation as 'a collaborative social interaction involving the exchange of words, gestures, sounds and signs in order to contribute to a common creative aim or joint activity of imagination or creation of novel behaviour, activity, artwork or artefact'. Such a conversation may involve many types of activity or behaviour, including humour, pretence and narrative, visual, auditory and musical representations. Each contribution to the conversation is not necessarily novel as such. The conversation or process itself is the creation. Fawcett and Hay (2004), who have developed their ideas from those of Craft and also the work at Reggio Emilia (alluded to elsewhere in this book), describe an exciting project involving collaboration between artists and schools: 'The whole process of children's explorations, thinking, representation and discussions is the focus, not the final product' (Craft 2003: 238). Thus, children and adults can build the activity through many types of conversational contribution, including responsive imitation as well as novel connections and initiation. The principal aim is collaboration through connectedness.

What do we know about the nature of the development of the child's creativity in collaboration with others? The best known and most obvious example of children's joint imagination and creativity, is interactive pretend play. Pretend play can be seen as a natural form of creativity 'a symbolic behaviour charged with feelings and emotional intensity, in which one thing is playfully treated as something else' (Fein 1981) Pretence involves the setting aside of current reality and stepping into the world of what could be. Social interactive pretence involves conversational collaboration with others to create this alternative world – making choices, sharing ideas, initiating and responding, taking into account the mental states and feelings of others.

The fullest behavioural evidence of this activity, role taking in pretend play, develops from the age of 12 months onwards and shows dramatic increases in frequency and complexity between the ages of 18 and 36 months (Howes 1987; Howes and Matheson 1992) and is in evidence in schools, playgrounds and families during the primary school years. This play allows children to set aside the current reality and to act and try out the parts of others from everyday or fantasy worlds, constructing a narrative in the process. Engel (2005) adds somewhat to our conceptions of pretend play when she suggests that young children use narrative play and stories to construct two types of fictional worlds – the worlds of 'what is', the world of plausible make-believe that simulates everyday life, and of 'what if', the world of more fantastic possibilities. She contends that 'what if' narratives, first enacted in pretend play and later spoken in the form of stories, provide children with a vehicle for experimenting with different kinds of non-reality. Children are thus able to compare real and the fantasy worlds and understand more fully the imaginative properties belonging to both types of world.

> An examination of the language young children use to accompany their narrative play and to tell stories demonstrates the ways in which children exploit the narrative form to contrast, compare, and traverse the constructed worlds of *what is* and *what if.*
>
> (Engel 2005: 514)

Additionally, we should note here that some writers contend that pretend play is a life-span activity, as vital for creative adult functioning as it is for young children's development, enabling us to develop representations of experiences with affective significance in a free, spontaneous, social, imaginative, fun and improvisational world – a process leading to the construction of knowledge and awareness about self and its relationship to the community (Goncu and Perone 2005).

Many studies also indicate the importance of role play in providing children with opportunities for planning and discussion in cooperation with their peers. This type of play interaction requires an awareness of others' desires and intentions and an ability to resolve conflicts, to crystallise choices and fantasies. At the same time the child can try out alternatives in a relatively protected sphere where playfulness is the order of the day and creative behaviour is normal. The playful nature of such conversations helps to release the child from anxiety as to the consequences of participation. As Tenenbaum et al. (2008:

252) succinctly state, the 'collaborative nature of conversations supports children in their zone of proximal development to engage at a higher level of reasoning and problem-solving than when alone'.

What, then, is the role of the adult, be they parent, care giver or teacher, in the process of this creative conversation? If we consider interactive pretence in the light of our theme of creative conversations, it is clear from many studies that play with more sophisticated partners such as older siblings or adults extends and elaborates the creativity of the pretence. Neilsen and Christie (2008) have shown that adult modelling of pretend acts increased the number of novel pretend acts of children between the ages of 27 and 41 months, catalysing their pretence. Bornstein and Tamis-LeMonda (1995), in their review of this area, provide convincing evidence relating to the role of adults in extending and elaborating symbolic role play with their children, channelling it towards greater complexity and sophistication.

Although I have stressed the significance of pretend role play as the commonest naturally occurring evidence of a child's creativity, it is important here to take a further step back and consider other types of development and interaction which are linked with and indeed provide an important basis for collaborative pretence. Possibly the earliest imaginative activity of the child is to imagine the emotions and thoughts of others. A considerable body of research and theory has built up over the last three decades relating to the role of interaction between care giver and child in the development of a representation of the self and other, their sense of the importance of their own mental life and its representations and imaginations, and the difference between the representations and imaginations of self and those of the other. This research has also shown how these interactions may enable children to develop a secure and valued sense of self and a sense of the efficacy of their actions – the feeling that he or she has a role in creating the world around. Key names in this research are Bowlby (1969; 1973), Trevarthen (Trevarthen and Aitken 2001), and Bruner (1968). Bowlby in many ways has set a major framework with his work on attachment, which has been succeeded by a wealth of research into attachment styles and their origins in care giver–child interaction. This has led on to more in-depth studies of the parameters and consequences of reciprocity in adult–child interactions.

Much work on care giver–child interaction has also stemmed from the ideas of Colwyn Trevarthen, who has posited and demonstrated the innate emotional underpinnings of infant–care giver interaction, its rhythmical and musical nature. Trevarthen particularly stresses the importance of emotion in all communications, asserting that human feelings and sensitivities 'form the dynamic texture of all live communication and experiencing together'. Trevarthen and Aitken (2001), in a fascinating review of the area, show how analyses of the *proto-conversations* between care giver and infant demonstrate that 'the specific rhythmic hierarchy of motor impulses shown in infantile vocalisations and spontaneous body movements, correspond to syllables, utterances, and phrases in the patterns of adult speech and music' (p. 24). They suggest that these are innate psychological features that enable infants and adults to interact efficiently by exchanging 'complementary, mutually-imitative, time-regulated messages, in synchrony or in alternation' (p. 24).

Bruner, following in the footsteps of Vygotsky (1962; 1978) has created an understanding of the role of playful interaction between care giver and child as laying the foundations of language and verbal conversation. Reciprocity and responsiveness to the child's contributions in interaction are seen as the keys to the child's development of a sense of self-worth and agency in the world, as a creator of change whose role in interaction is valued. More recently, researchers have also shown the key role conversation plays within the family in the development of the child's understanding of self and others (de Rosnay and Hughes 2006). It has, moreover, been clearly shown that the level of the ability to imagine the self and mental states of others is closely linked to the connectedness between conversational participants and the extent to which feelings and mental states are mentioned or discussed within a family (Hughes et al. 2006). This body of theory and research has also led us to understand more fully the role of others – adults and more competent peers and siblings – as cultural 'teachers', mentors and partners in the creation of individual understanding of the world and development of a role in the world. So reciprocity and connectedness in conversations between adults and children are seen to be the most important elements in creating imaginative perspective taking with others. Relationships of trust are also an important aspect of the environment for these conversations. Children must feel that their contributions are valued, their voice heard, and that there is no judgement about their correctness. They are part of a shared experience. If we turn again to the adult's role in interacting with the child in pretend play we find that 'interactions that are responsive to children's expressed interests serve to extend and elaborate symbolic engagements, inculcate feelings of self-efficacy and mobilize children's further exploration of and learning about the environment' (Bornstein and Tamis-LeMonda 1995: 391). On the other hand, it must be noted that 'intrusive behaviours, including attempts to shift the child's focus away from a topic of interest, are unrelated or inversely related to advances in such abilities' (ibid.: 392).

What skills does the creative conversation require of the adult if s/he is to participate fully and provide the environment that fosters creativity in children? First, we can consider verbal interaction with the child, since, as many researchers have shown, 'Adults' conversational styles directly affect children's ability and willingness to actively participate in conversations in a manner that is child rather than adult driven' (Lamb and Brown 2006: 227). Skilled communication is clearly one of the most important of teacher skills. Research into children's development shows us that particular aspects of adult behaviour in interaction with children serve to promote their cognitive development, language, conversational competence, narrative skills and the understanding of others' contributions (Girolametto and Weitzman 2002 2007; Griffiths 2002; Siraj-Blatchford and Sylva 2004; Dunn 2006; Ensor and Hughes 2008; Tomasello and Farrar 1986; Tenenbaum et al. 2008). These aspects are:

- use of appropriate types of questioning and other speech acts;
- sensitive responding to interests/focus/concerns of children;
- acceptance of all contributions;
- allowance of time for the child to respond;
- valuing of imitation of children and by children;
- connectedness to children's concerns and communication;
- use of mentalistic and emotional explanations and discussions.

An interesting illustration of one of the many sources of evidence relating to these points comes from the work of Robyn Fivush and others on the development of the child's ability to remember and narrate stories from past experience. Thus, many research studies by Fivush and others have shown that parents who use open-ended questions, repeat children's responses and follow their children's lead in conversations have children who provide more elaborative narratives about past events (e.g. Fivush et al. 2006; Fivush and Nelson 2006; Fivush 2007).

In relation to creativity, Craft and colleagues show the importance of the type of questions we use, in her work on the development of 'possibility thinking' in children (Chappell et al. 2008). Possibility thinking (PT) is described as focusing on posing the question 'What if?' in multiple ways, and involving the shift from asking 'What is this and what does it do?' to 'What can I do with this?', particularly in relation to identifying, honing and solving problems. Craft defines three type of question: 1) leading questions, which provide the overarching framework, or main question for possibility thinking; 2) service questions, which are those posed in the service of the leading question in order to move the PT forward in relation to responding to the leading question; 3) follow-through questions, which frame the minute detail of the final-stage activities that achieve outcomes of PT, whether concrete or abstract. She provides evidence from a study of children aged between 3 and 6 years of how such question posing and question responding were used by both children and adults, and drive the shift from 'what is' to 'what might be' within possibility thinking, and in turn creative learning.

The foregoing summary of research into conversational collaboration and creative activity leads me to suggest that the shared nature of conversations may support the child's creativity in several ways:

- by conversational connectedness: prompting and valuing imaginative, novel, divergent and elaborative responses;
- by open-ended questioning, connecting to the child's perspective/point of view, imitating the child's response, giving the child time to respond, enhancing child's vocabulary relating to the activity and encouraging reflection on and sharing of experiences;
- valuing the child's self-expression (not correcting or denigrating) and developing the child's sense of agency and efficacy;
- encouraging and facilitating natural exchange between peers which may allow perspective taking and imagination through such types of interaction as conflict, pretence and emotional exchange;
- serving as a source of information as to the cultural values of their socio-cultural community.

Wider adult roles

The teacher and other adults in the classroom have of course a wider role to play over and above that of interacting verbally with children. Findings from research over a ten-year period have been well summarised by Lobman, who explains that research studies in classrooms have found that, in the best learning environments,

> teachers elaborate and enhance children's learning by adding to the activity at hand, and are therefore able to help take it to a new level. These teachers do more than prepare for, observe, and monitor children; they take part in their activities by

> joining in as co-participants and by adding materials and information when it is needed. They are sensitive to what children are doing, and do not change the subject or distract children away from their pursuits. When teachers do give directions it follows from what the children are already engaged in, or introduces uninvolved children to new activities.
>
> (Lobman 2006: 455)

Children come from many different places into one classroom. They come with different understandings of who they are and what is permitted in life. For some there is anxiety, for others lack of understanding, for others lack of physical development, for others lack of social cognition. We can see that for all these children there will be a place in group collaborative conversation as long as all contributions are valued and supportiveness of others is the frame. Some interesting accounts of the value of this type of collaboration can be found in teachers' evaluation of the Reggio Emilia approach as allowing inclusion of children with special needs (Gilman 2007) and as allowing full participation of children from different linguistic backgrounds (Fraser 2007).

As the chapters in this book demonstrate, being child centred does not entail of necessity letting the children take charge and follow their own agenda with disregard for others. As several writers here explain, the teacher's role is to create an environment that allows the child to make choices and explore. A good example of this has been described in Fawcett and Hay (2004), where the introduction of a creative project, based on the principles of Reggio Emilia, was seen to effect significant changes in the environments of whole schools and nurseries. However, in terms of objective research, little is known about the outcomes for such creative approaches in education. The creative process may be documented and researched as part of the ongoing education and development of children and teachers, as in the Reggio Emilia programme (e.g. Rinaldi 2006; Edwards et al. 1998) but the effects of such regimes on children's lives are yet to be understood. Clearly, any educational regime is developed and embedded in a wider socio-cultural environment. The current press for a return to creative approaches (see Gibson 2005) indicates that creativity is valued for both its social and economic benefits. The essentially Vygotskyian social constructivism described here will perhaps give new life to our education systems.

Conclusions

In summary, the following conclusions can be drawn from the research and theory cited here. Conversational collaborations provide the ideal environment for children to develop their creativity of self-expression. Children come to the nursery or classroom pre-wired to learn from others but having already been party to formative experiences within their families that will shape their willingness and competence as a contributor. The model of conversation provided for them will shape their further competencies. Adults have a key role to play in enabling children to extend and elaborate their creativity in collaborative conversation, in which creativity should first of all be valued as a process rather than as a product. Imitation is an important part of collaboration. Adults need to be involved in responding creatively – not just to be acting out a pre-written role. Adults' understanding of child development will radically affect the roles they adopt as teachers.

Reading and resources

Bohanek, J.G., Marin, K.A., Fivush, R. and Duke, M.P. (2006) 'Family narrative interaction and children's sense of self', *Family Process* 45 (1), 39–54.

Bornstein, M.H. and Tamis-LeMonda, C.S. (1995) 'Parent-child symbolic play – 3 theories in search of an effect', *Developmental Review* 15 (4), 382–400.

Bornstein, M.H., Tamis-LeMonda, C.S. and Haynes, O.M. (1999) 'First words in the second year: continuity, stability, and models of concurrent and predictive correspondence in vocabulary and verbal responsiveness across age and context', *Infant Behavior & Development* **22** (1), 65–85.

Bowlby, J. (1969) *Attachment and Loss, Vol. 1: Attachment*, London: Hogarth Press and the Institute of Psycho-Analysis.

——(1973) *Attachment and Loss, Vol. 2: Separation: Anxiety and anger*, London: Hogarth Press and Institute of Psycho-Analysis.

Bruner, J. (1968) *Processes of Cognitive Growth: infancy*, vol. III, Heinz Warner Lecture Series, Worcester, MA: Clark University Press.

Carpenter, M., Nagell, K. and Tomasello, M. (1998) 'Social cognition, joint attention, and communicative competence from 9 to 15 months of age', *Child Development* 63 (4), i–vi, 1–143.

Chappell, K., Craft, A., Burnard, P. and Cremin, T. (2008) 'Question-posing and question-responding: the heart of "Possibility Thinking" in the early years', *Early Years* 28 (3), 267–86.

Clark, E.V. and Bernicot, J. (2008) 'Repetition as ratification: How parents and children place information in common ground', *Journal of Child Language* 35 (2), 349–71.

Craft, A. (2003) 'The limits to creativity in education: dilemmas for the educator', *British Journal Of Educational Studies* 51 (2), 113–27.

Craft, A. and Jeffrey, B. (2008) 'Creativity and performativity in teaching and learning: tensions, dilemmas, constraints, accommodations and synthesis', *British Educational Research Journal* 34 (5), 577–84.

de Rosnay, M. and Hughes, C. (2006) 'Conversation and theory of mind: Do children talk their way to socio-cognitive understanding?', *British Journal of Developmental Psychology* 24, 7–37, Part 1.

Dunn, J. (2006) 'A discussion of the Merrill-Palmer Quarterly special issue', *Merrill-Palmer Quareterly Journal of Developmental Psychology*, 52 (1)151–7.

Edwards, C. P., Gandini, L. and Forman, G. (1998) *The Hundred Languages of Children: The Reggio Emilia approach to early childhood education*, Norwood, NJ: Ablex Publishing.

Engel, S. (2005) 'The narrative worlds of what is and what if', *Cognitive Development* **20** (4), 514–25.

Ensor, R. and Hughes, C. (2008) 'Content or connectedness? Mother-child talk and early social understanding', *Child Development* 79 (1), 201–16.

Farmer, M. (2002) 'Social interactionism in practice: a review', in F. Griffiths (ed.) *Communication Counts: speech and language difficulties in the early years*, London: David Fulton Publishers.

Fawcett, M. and Hay, P. (2004) '5x5x5 = creativity in the early years', *International Journal of Art & Design Education* 23 (3), 234–45.

Fein, G.G. (1981) 'Pretend play in childhood: an integrative review', *Child Development* **52**, 1095–1118.

Fivush, R. (2007) 'Maternal reminiscing style and children's developing understanding of self and emotion', *Clinical Social Work Journal* 35 (1), 37–46.

Fivush, R. and Nelson, K. (2006) 'Parent–child reminiscing locates the self in the past', *British Journal of Developmental Psychology* 24, 235–51.

Fivush, R., Haden, C.A. and Reese, E. (2006) 'Elaborating on elaborations: role of maternal reminiscing style in cognitive and socioemotional development', *Child Development* **77** (6), 1568–88.

Fraser, S. (2007) 'Play in other languages', *Theory Into Practice* 46 (1), 14ff.

Gibson, H. (2005) 'What creativity isn't: the presumptions of instrumental and individual justifications for creativity in education', *British Journal of Educational Studies* 53 (2), 148–67.

Gilman, S. (2007) 'Including the child with special needs: learning from Reggio Emilia', *Theory Into Practice* 46 (1), 23ff.

Girolametto, L. and Weitzman, E. (2002) 'Responsiveness of child care providers in interactions with toddlers and preschoolers', *Language Speech and Hearing Services in Schools* 33 (4), 268–81.

Girolametto, L. and Weitzman, E. (2007) 'Promoting peer interaction skills – Professional development for early childhood educators and preschool teachers', *Topics in Language Disorders* 27 (2), 93–110.

Girolametto, L., Weitzman, E. and Greenberg, J. (2004) 'The effects of verbal support strategies on small-group peer interactions', *Language Speech and Hearing Services in Schools* **35** (3), 254–68.

Goncu, A. and Perone, A. (2005) 'Pretend play as a life-span activity', *Topoi* 24, 137–47.

Grice, H.P. (1975) 'Logic and conversation', in P. Cole and J.L. Morgan (eds), *Syntax and Semantics,* Volume 3, *Speech acts,* pp. 41–58, New York: Academic Press.

Griffiths, F. (2002) *Communication Counts: speech and language difficulties in the early years,* London: David Fulton Publishers.

Henzi, S.P., Pereira, L.F.D.S., Hawker-Bond, D., Stiller, J., Dunbar, R.I.M. and Barrett, L. (2007) 'Look who's talking: developmental trends in the size of conversational cliques', *Evolution and Human Behavior* 28 (1), 66–74.

Howes, C. (1987) 'Social competence with peers in young-children – developmental sequences', *Developmental Review* 7 (3), 252–72.

Howes, C. and Matheson, C.C. (1992) 'Sequences in the development of competent play with peers – social and social pretend play', *Developmental Psychology* 28 (5), 961–74.

Hughes, C., Fujisawa, K.K., Ensor, R., Lecce, S. and Marfleet, R. (2006) 'Cooperation and conversations about the mind', *British Journal of Developmental Psychology* 24 (1), 53–72.

Hurley, S., Clark, A. and Kiverstein, J. (2008) 'The shared circuits model (SCM): how control, mirroring, and simulation can enable imitation, deliberation, and mindreading', *Behavioral and Brain Sciences* 31 (1), 1ff.

Lamb, M.E. and Brown, D.A. (2006) 'Conversational apprentices: Helping children become competent informants about their own experiences', *British Journal of Developmental Psychology* 24, 215–34, Part 1.

Lobman, C.L. (2006) 'Improvisation: an analytic tool for examining teacher–child interactions in the early childhood classroom', *Early Childhood Research Quarterly*, 21, 455–70.

McEwen, F., Happe, F., Bolton, P., Rijsdijk, F., Ronald, A., Dworzynski, K. and Plomin, R. (2007) 'Origins of individual differences in imitation: Links with language, pretend play, and socially insightful behavior in two-year-old twins', *Child Development* 78 (2), 474–92.

Neilsen, M. and Christie,T. (2008) 'Adult modelling facilitates young children's generation of pretend acts', *Infant & Child Development* 17 (2), 151–62.

Nicely, P., Tamis-LeMonda, C.S. and Bornstein, M.H. (1999) 'Mothers' attuned responses to infant affect expressivity promote earlier achievement of language milestones', *Infant Behavior & Development* 22 (4), 557–68.

Ninio, A. and Snow, C. (1999) 'The development of pragmatics: Learning to use language appropriately', in T.K. Bhatia and W.C. Ritchie (eds), *Handbook of Language Acquisition*, pp. 347–83, New York: Academic Press.

Rinaldi, C. (2006) *In Dialogue with Reggio Emilia*, London: Routledge.

Siegal, M. (1999) 'Language and thought: the fundamental significance of conversational awareness for cognitive development', *Developmental Science* **2** (1), 1–14.

Siraj-Blatchford, I. and Sylva, K. (2004) 'Researching pedagogy in English pre-schools', *British Educational Research Journal* 30 (5), 713–30.

Tenenbaum, H.R., Alfieri, L., Brooks, P.J. and Dunne, G. (2008) 'The effects of explanatory conversations on children's emotion understanding', *British Journal of Developmental Psychology* 26, 249–63.

Tomasello, M. and Farrar, M. (1986) 'Joint attention and early language', *Child Development* 57, 1454–63.

Trevarthen, C. and Aitken, K.J. (2001) 'Infant intersubjectivity: research, theory, and clinical applications', *Journal of Child Psychology and Psychiatry* 42, 3–48.

Vygotsky, L.S. (1978) *Mind in Society: the development of higher psychological processes*, Cambridge, MA: Harvard University Press.

——(1962) *Thought and Language*, Cambridge, MA: MIT Press.

Weblinks

Early Education
www.early-education.org.uk

National Children's Bureau
www.ncb.org.uk

Sightlines (ReggioUKnetwork)
www.sightlines-initiative.com

Index

Supporting Children's Creativity Through Music, Dance, Drama and Art

There is a growing awareness in Early Years education that an essential part of children's development involves creative engagement through language, gestures, body movements, drawing and music; creating shared meanings in playful contexts.

Supporting Children's Creativity through Music, Dance, Drama and Art brings together contributions from a range of professionals and early years practitioners, to help readers implement the themes of the Early Years Foundation Stage framework in a creative way. Emphasising the need for responsive adults and a creative atmosphere for learning, this book covers:

- How to promote a creative classroom effectively
- The importance of talking and listening in groups
- Working with community artists
- Music making and story telling in the classroom
- Practical resources and theoretical grounding
- Making use of the 'Talking Table' technique

With practical case studies drawn from a range of contexts, this book highlights the contribution that creativity makes to children's learning and social development, illustrated through practical suggestions and feedback from tried and tested methods.

Appealing to all with an interest in Early Years practice, this book demonstrates how practitioners can put excitement and inspiration back into the learning process, and guides them to encourage and support the creative capacities of young children.

Fleur Griffiths is a retired nursery teacher/educational psychologist/senior lecturer in Early Childhood Studies at Sunderland University. In retirement she has worked on a contract basis as an educational consultant in Foundation Stage settings in local authorities. She has also contributed to the delivery of CPD training for teachers in Hartlepool.